W9-AFS-124

The Truth is Concrete

The Truth
is Concrete

by
DOROTHEE SOLLE

Translated by DINAH LIVINGSTONE

Theodore Lownik Library
Illinois Benedictine College
Lisle, Illinois 60532

London · Burns & Oates

BURNS & OATES LIMITED
25 Ashley Place, London, S.W.1

First published 1969

This is a translation of Die Wahrheit ist konkret, *first published by Walter-Verlag, Olten, 1967*

© Walter-Verlag AG, Olten, 1967
English translation © Burns & Oates Ltd, 1969
SBN: 223 30050 0

Made and printed in Great Britain by
Billing & Sons Limited
Guildford and London

Contents

Foreword

When Brecht was in exile in Denmark he had on his study wall the motto I have taken for the title of this book. It is an old sentence derived from Hegel by the Marxist tradition and now part of its wisdom. In Lenin it reads: "This is the foundation of the dialectic: there is no such thing as abstract truth; truth is always concrete." This principle is in harmony with the Christian notion of truth, or at least that Christian notion which I hold. It dismisses the view that truth is simply *there* and can be given unchanging expression. It considers the situations in which people live and the needs they feel. It does not forget the oppressed. For these determine our truth. Christianity sees the truth as concrete, historical and partisan.

When Christ said to Pilate that the truth is concrete, this late Roman sceptic answered with the famous question, "What is truth?" (Jn 18.37). It is a rhetorical question on two levels. On one level it expresses a philosophical scepticism, but denying only abstract knowledge. However deep his doubt may have been about this, it did not touch the concrete truth of his way of life, his position, his income, etc. For on the other level Pilate knew his own concrete truth very well. He was power and it was against this power and its scepticism that Christ set his own particular truth, love.

Christ's truth is concrete. That is what this book is about. This is the sole reason for demythologizing the Bible, reforming the Church and changing society. By concrete we mean changeable according to the situation and according to human needs; able itself to change a situation and liberate from

7

oppression. This kind of truth must be realized and so it can be experienced but it cannot be known in advance. It can be made but not determined. And so this book is dedicated to my readers.

While preparing this book for press I tried to imagine my possible reader. He is a Christian frustrated by the Church. He examines the possibilities of Christian life outside the Church. The images of Christian life which he is offered bewilder him. For he is denied the means to put his Christianity into practice. To him, doctrine and liturgy, the institution and its para- phernalia, seem remote, they are strange and thwart his wishes. I have at any rate had many letters expressing this sort of disappointment.* People have hopes but they remain unexpressed.

Anyone who wants to express these hopes must try to describe his own experiences. I use the word "experiences" on purpose. It is usually used about sexual experiences. This has a good reason. One person's sexual experiences cannot replace another's. Everyone has to go through it all for himself. If anyone objects to this usage of the word let me refer him to the mystics. They tried to express their lives in sexual language, and spoke of making love, conception and birth. They found it a good language because it was fit to express their own deepest and most private experiences.

Our language has the unfortunate expression "an experi- enced woman", whose unpleasant connotation fails to suggest that experiences can be revolutionary. "Experiences" might as well be cars, pictures, books or ties which are possessed. Our relationship to the world is devitalized, desexualized we might say, because we so seldom take the other seriously enough for us in turn to be taken seriously. This seriousness is what we are talking about. Experiences are the way to self-knowledge.

* The material in this book was originally presented as a series of radio talks.

Faith and hope are to help us on this way. But here I must warn my reader that everything that I have written could be understood without mention of Christ. But I understand better with the help of Christ. That is all. This is the purpose of theology. By it my life becomes clearer and more conscious. "It does not yet appear what we shall be" (1 Jn 3.2). In my experience of particular truth I direct myself towards a self which does not yet exist.

I

Is God an Anachronism?

Some preachers make a point of beginning their Sunday
sermon with a joke. Though I hope the subject of this chapter,
the relation between Christian belief and scientific thought,
does not need such a device, I should nevertheless like to
begin with a joke as it leads us straight to the point. This
story comes from the Soviet Union.

"Thank God," said the peasant woman, "it is going to rain."

"But, Comrade," said the manager of the collective farm,
"you know very well that God doesn't exist, thank God."

"Of course, Comrade, but what if, which God forbid, he
did?"

You will have noticed that this is a double-level class of
joke. Indeed, we can distinguish three levels. The first is the
simple popular belief, the inherited custom, convention or
unthinking habit, which even convinced atheists do not always
lose, of bringing not only quotations from the Bible, but the
name of God himself into their conversation. This way of
talking is not far off superstition. God is our superterrestrial
old man who controls the clouds and air and wind and sends
or protects us from war, the pox and inflation. It is the child's
God who mends my broken dolly and changes the bad mark
in my exercise book into a good one on my way home from
school.

The second level is that of official Marxist propaganda.

Since 1917 there has been no God in the Soviet Union. Where could he live? In heaven? In the universe? Concern about God's dwelling place came to an end about four hundred years ago and, in the age of space flight, there is not even room for it in children's stories.

But, with the natural sciences flourishing, the Marxist critique of religion does not have to rely on this cheap point that God is homeless. What is more important is that there is nothing left for him to do. What indeed could he do? War and inflation are made by man and it is conceivable that man could cure them. They are no longer mysterious. We can protect ourselves against smallpox by vaccination and against hail by insurance. God is out of work as soon as man begins to think in a scientific way and orders his world according to scientific laws. There can be no such thing as a Christian science, for two and two make four for Christians just as they do for everyone else, including Marxists. The biologist researching into the origins of man cannot assume Christian dogma if he wants to be a proper scientist. He must have no such presuppositions. He does not know in advance that man comes "from God". He asks questions, investigates, researches and discusses independently of his religion. In this sense God has nothing to do with science, and as Christians we should be careful not to confine him to the regions as yet unprobed by it. For if that were his place he would indeed have been in retreat for the last four hundred years, a retreat about to turn into total flight.

For a long time religion served to explain the world, or rather it happened to serve this function. If this were the important thing about religion it would be true that this is a religionless age. If we expect religion to explain the world and think of it first and foremost as a set of doctrines to which we can give assent, we will have to admit that science is better at explaining the world. Modern non-Christians and post-Christians no longer need God. They do not need the Christian myth to explain the world, they look to science. In a novel written in 1960, *Halbzeit* by Martin Walser, a young woman writes in her diary:

> With Lissa in church. Could not pray. Official language sounded strange. Paraphernalia, vocabulary not my scene. Do people think God only listens when they say prayers and pays no attention when they just think or speak? Impossible to imagine the priest has experienced what he was talking about in the sermon. I cannot express my life any more in prayer language. Too much of a strain. I inherited God in these formulas but now I am losing him through them. He has become a sort of wizard with a queer magic language, an anachronism.

This God, a wizard who can no longer be taken seriously, has nowhere to go because the sky is not his dwelling place but a space through which we can travel. He is as irrelevant as the magic of the past. This past world cannot be recalled. Science and technology have destroyed it. It is an interesting historical question how this destruction of the former world could have come from the Christian West. Why didn't the other great religions, Buddhism, Confucianism, Islam, produce an enlightenment in this sense? Is this an accident? Or is there something in Christianity itself which required such a development? Is Christianity the religion which contains within it the doom of all religions, the necessary pilgrimage to the religionless state?

The creation story contains God's commission to man: Subdue the earth. In every ancient religion the earth is holy. She is worshipped as the earth mother. This commission has something horrifying about it. Dominate the earth mother! This is too bold. This is blasphemy. God himself commands man to destroy the ancient world, to shatter its deepest piety and throw out its most basic superstition. The God of the Bible himself commands man to overthrow the throne on which he sits. And this means that science is in no way the enemy of religion but its historical successor. The great movement of history which we call secularization is not in the least to be regretted. It actually arises from the Christian religion and Christian freedom in its attitude towards the world. Faith has nothing to fear from her grown-up son; she should rejoice at the achievements of science and technology. Whenever man enters into his dominion over the world, the gods may tremble who send the lightning and the hail, but our God has nothing to fear. Science can neither prove nor disprove him. Or would he be disproved if the missing link were discovered? In fact the God whom the Marxists attack, the God who loves darkness and childish ways, the God of superstition and un-enlightenment, would not be disproved. He has already been disproved, he is dead. But is he the God of Jesus Christ? The existence of trust in the world, which is at least as necessary as bread, and the existence of love, are not affected by science, satellites, evolutionary theory, artificial rain or anything else of that nature. We cannot measure this love and trust, and science is not able to decide whether or not they are what really count in our lives, the one reason not to give up in despair.

And so we come to the third level of our joke, at which God, God forbid, might exist. Not a God who explains the world and three thousand years ago wrote a book in order to do so. But a God who loves the world and wants us to love it too. And not love it merely in the exalted moments of our lives, but day after day.

We cannot salvage the first level, the level of childish faith at which science and religion are not distinguished. The

Marxist criticism reveals the inadequacy of this level and for this we should be grateful to it. Within its own limits the scientific view of the world is perfectly correct. It is criticizing not God but a pre-scientific way of looking at the world.

But the third level, the level at which we suspect and fear that there may none the less be a God, and that this God is right in what he expects of us, and that Jesus was telling the truth when he said that God wants us, crazy though it may sound, to trust in a world full of mistrust and hatred, this third level opens up a whole new dimension, the dimension of the truly human. Faith and science are not irreconcilable, as we can easily see if we substitute for "faith" and "hope", "trust" or "love". These are not disturbed by science and they are not possible without him who is found in them and makes them meaningful. This being who is found in trust, and who sets at the centre of life an attitude whose consequences cannot be measured or calculated, is not I, is not "mankind" or its "highest ideal", but what Christians call God.

And what if, which God forbid, this God existed? It would be dangerous for our world in which everything is calculable except our fellow man. It would be dangerous because we would have to revise our standards. For we would be bringing the unknown into our arithmetic. And this unknown could not be relegated to the position of a pseudo-science but it would be at the centre of our lives. Our lives can fail and be irrelevant, because God exists; or they can succeed as a human project, because God exists.

2

We have no Pride, only Interests

Nikita Kruschchev was once reported as saying: "We have no pride, only interests." The paper in which I read this remark called this undignified. Is it not right for a man to be proud? To be aware of his dignity? But I remembered a story from the New Testament which is about someone who had no pride, only interests.

She is a woman and we know almost nothing about her. We only have two facts. She lives in Gentile country, that is to say in Syro-Palestine. Matthew describes her as a Canaanite woman, an old-fashioned description with a religious reference. But the point he is making for his story is simply that she does not have the right hymnbook, she is a pagan. Secondly we know that she has a daughter. We do not know how old the woman is, whether she has a husband living, how long her daughter has been ill or with what disease, or what means of support the two of them have. This woman has heard of the famous miracle worker from Nazareth, and she knows that in Israel people are asking whether he is the expected prince and saviour or whether he is a fraud. For herself she thinks he is genuine, he is the promised and long awaited one.

The story begins like this. The woman sees the famous man in the street and seizes her opportunity without bothering whether she is disturbing him. As it happens he has retired to this Gentile country to withdraw from the publicity surrounding him in Israel. But how is she to know that? She sees him and runs after him trying to attract his attention. The famous man walks on, taking no notice as the woman cries after him to have pity on her. On her? But it is her daughter who is ill! The woman is unaware of such niceties. Her daughter's distress is her own. If no one helps her daughter, no one has pity on her. She does what she does in her own interest. She does not say "Have pity on my daughter" but "Have pity on me". She does not shrink from calling the famous man by his royal title, Son of David, and she cries after him in the street to tell him how sick her daughter is.

Have you ever spoken to people in the street who simply took no notice? Who did not even look at you, or speak, but went on walking as if you did not exist? And what did *you* do when this happened?

But this is just the beginning, someone asks for help in the street and someone else ignores it. Perhaps the woman's neighbours came out to watch the stranger and the humiliation of the "woman with the sick daughter", and were mildly excited and pleased by her pain, each one going home with the comfortable feeling that this could not happen to me, because *I* have my pride. If I was in her position I would suffer in silence. . . .

But the woman took no notice and continued to cry after him. She made such a commotion that his companions tried to silence her. It was unpleasant to be bothered by a woman like her out in the street. "Tell her to be quiet", they said to their master, who had said nothing. They were a bit annoyed and a bit distressed by her and so they said, "She is shrieking at us". They had as much pity as we might have for a beggar who will not leave us until we get to our own front door.

She tried again and was again rejected. The famous man told his companions that he had not come for everyone but only for the people with the right hymnbook. Why he said this and whether he really did say it, I do not want to discuss here. We are not for the moment interested in him but, like the narrator, in the woman. Eventually her case is discussed.

Perhaps you have been discussed in your presence without anyone taking any notice of you. It is simple courtesy not to speak "about" someone when he is present without speaking "to" him.

But courtesy apart, do you remember what Kruschchev said? Then you can see that the woman did not then do the proper and dignified thing, she did not go home.

On the contrary she came nearer to the famous man, fell on her knees and said simply: "Lord, help me." Was this sensible? While the famous man's friends were on her side, perhaps she had a chance. But when they were against her? There was no one left to help her, she was on her own. How long is it sensible to hope? Until the other person says plainly, "I won't". But wasn't that what he had been thinking all along? She is not interested in what he is thinking or what he wants. That he seems to be hostile, that he is not noticing her, perhaps despising her, the attitude of his disciples, are not her concern. She minds about her daughter.

This is her most humiliating attempt. She falls on her knees before him who has treated her like a dog. The famous man has said that he has only come to help a certain people and she could have said, "What a pity I am not a Jew". Instead of which she says, "Help me".

Someone who has a real interest at heart cannot afford resignation any more than pride. Now the famous man brings it to an issue. He has dealt her three "mortal blows", as Luther puts it; he has kept silence, he has refused her request as impossible and now he compares her to a dog. "It is not right to give the children's bread to the dogs." The dog was considered the most despised and miserable of creatures.

Even if we follow the story up till now, I do not mean the harsh behaviour of Jesus but the woman's behaviour, what happens next seems to me quite crazy. One could also say it is holy. For she still does not do the proper thing, lower her head and agree with him. Everything that has happened tells against her image of him as a kind man and saviour who loves mankind. But she does not let her image be destroyed, she remembers what she wants and thinks (as Luther puts it), "Do what you like, I will still go on believing that what I first thought was true". Even when the contrary seems self-evident, and he is cold and rude, she does not bother about her feelings or her reputation, she does not despair but answers him in his own terms.

She says, "But, Lord, the dogs eat the crumbs that fall from their master's table". She accepts Jesus' judgment which threatens to destroy all her hope, stays on her knees and with all the presence of mind she can muster seeks to catch him in his own words. She accepts that she has no right to be helped, no claim on him and that all she can do is beg. It no longer matters to her what her behaviour looks like.

This fourth and last attempt—first calling and running after him, then asking the disciples, then falling on her knees and now this acceptance of his harsh judgment—achieves her end. Jesus gives in and tells her that her daughter will be healed.

We have no pride, only interests. Jesus expresses it differently and means exactly that: "Woman, great is your faith." We have heard aright and Kruschchev's attitude is a Christian one whatever his intentions. The faith which Jesus praises to the people is simply to have no more pride, only a single interest. What is this interest? I think the saints behaved like the woman in our story, paying no attention to their own feelings and without self-consciousness. Without fear for themselves. They are too afraid of something else to have time to be frightened for themselves. They are interested in something outside themselves, says Brecht about "good people".

Our interest can either be in ourself or in something outside ourself. The proud man is interested in himself, he minds what he looks like to other people and is therefore never completely involved in what he is doing but has one eye on himself. He is not free to give himself completely to what he is trying to do.

The interest which is free from pride is in something outside myself. He who has no pride, only interests, becomes uninteresting to himself. His own feelings are no longer his ultimate concern. "God is greater than our heart" and we can let something that we feel acutely pass as unimportant. Listen once more to Luther who was very fond of this story. "The woman is thinking of God. Do what you like. Call me dog, cat, rat, mouse, I do not care. Were the angel Gabriel to come down from heaven it would be nothing to me. I must take care of my daughter."

This attitude which can bear any humiliation, because it is no longer interested in itself, has from the beginning been given a name by Christians which is over-used but still great and beautiful, a word which you may have noticed has not been used in our story, the word "freedom".

3
Why does Theology change?

If the subject of theology was God and God alone, throned above the cherubim, it would be a science that must content itself with the repetition of eternally true statements. There could be disagreements, but these would all have been settled in the early centuries and theology, in the Western sense of a living, changing and arguable science, would long ago have ceased to exist. In fact there is a form of Christianity where this is the case, the Orthodox Church. It has remained untouched by the *Zeitgeist*, unchanging and timeless in its expression of the truth given once and for all.

This is not so with us. The older people among us will need all the fingers of their hand to count the different theologies that have been current during their lifetime, and there is no end to change. There can be two explanations for this fact. Either the subject of theology is not God but human conceptions of him and wishes projected upon the other world which pass for supernatural science. Or it is the will of God that theology should change, because theology is not about him as a heavenly being but about man his care. If it is about man, this can only mean that it is about real, changing historical man. Theology must change or else it would be meaningless. It must distinguish between the world view of a particular period and faith, between legend and fact, past mythology and present existence. It must change because it must be about man or else it could not speak of God at all. For it cannot speak of God in general and in eternal formulas which are independent of our faith in him. For we can only say about God what he does to us.

Ever since modern science has affected our view of things, many people have found it impossible to take the Bible as it stands, particularly the miracle stories. A so-called supernatural understanding which maintains that "it happened like this and you must believe it" makes the Bible a collection of fairy stories, Jesus a magician and the Christian a schizophrenic living in two irreconcilable worlds, a mysterious religious world and a causally explicable ordinary world. The contradictions between these two worlds, the religious and the scientific, have forced theologians to develop the various forms of biblical criticism, for example to try to understand the story of the feeding of the five thousand when it is no longer possible to take it as it stands. What are we to make of the story that Jesus fed with five loaves and two fishes five thousand people, or according to another tradition four thousand or another five thousand not counting the women and children, which might make eight thousand?

At first biblical criticism tried to explain it in this way. The Order of Essenes, with whom Jesus was connected, left a large stock of bread in a hole. Jesus stood by the secret opening to the hole and handed out loaf after loaf and gave them to the disciples to give to the multitude.

Another explanation suggests that Jesus said to his disciples about the hungry people: "We want to give a good example to the rich" and began to share his and his disciples' food with those sitting next to him. The example worked and everybody was given enough. On their own the people would never have shared their bread. They would have fought over it and done each other harm, as they have done since the world began and will do till its end. When they saw him, the son of man, they remembered that they were all brothers and children of one father. They understood that "mine" and "yours" means death, "mine is yours" means life.

This liberal explanation of the miracle throws light on the story and shows us Jesus as a human being—and yet it does not do justice to the text or to what the author intended. Jesus is not as easily understood or as close to us as the liberal version would have it.

The second stage of the critical development is the school of history of religions. It places our story in its religious context, it notes many parallels with other religions between this and nearly all the miracle stories. Miraculous food, healing of the sick, power over natural forces such as wind, fire and water, virgin birth and resurrection from the dead are ascribed, with the same conviction, the same claims and no less credibility to other religious heroes. To name only Greco-Latin ones, Heracles, Alexander the Great, Augustus. Why should we trust the witness of the New Testament more than other sources, when the history of religions shows clearly that certain themes crop up frequently and are applied as readily to one hero as to another?

Miraculous multiplication of food is one such theme. It often appears in the Old Testament and here it is applied to Jesus, the fulfilment of the promises, without there necessarily being a historical basis to the story. This second explanation of the story is thus not really an explanation at all but a solution to it: it is a borrowed legend.

Criticism did not rest content with this answer. It continued to ask questions and this led to a third stage. Why is this story told about Jesus? What is its purpose? What was the intention of the primitive community when it transferred this borrowed theme to Jesus? What is characteristic of Jesus in the story? The miraculous multiplication of the loaves is a reference to

the Last Supper and thus to the kingdom of God. It's point
is not the satisfaction of hunger but the sitting down to table
with Jesus. The sharers in his supper are the citizens of his
kingdom, this is what the story is saying.

This method of criticism maintains the presupposition of
the historical critical analysis which holds that the story is
not about the life of Jesus as it actually happened, but a later
post-Easter tradition. This negative side is not, however, the
whole story. History cannot rest content with it.

History must have the historical fact. Miraculous multiplication of loaves is a theme which may be very interesting to the
student of myth, but Christian faith cannot rest on the faithful
acceptance of this or that legend which appears in the New
Testament. History can only be satisfied if it actually happened.

But the authors of the New Testament were not concerned
only with the publication of factual information. What they
wanted was simply this: to preach Jesus. They wanted to say
what Jesus was about. They told what they had been through
with him. They expressed it in the images, themes and modes
of thought that they found to hand. They spoke—this is an
obvious fact which I would not have to mention if its consequences were also as obvious—the language of their time and
not a heavenly language. It was a language in which one could
say with perfect seriousness Mr Smith has bewitched my pig
or Mrs Jones has the evil eye. Did the evangelists tell their
stories to say that Jesus can work magic? They assumed this
in transferring the borrowed magical themes to him. But this
was not the most important thing about him. They wanted
to say what they had heard from Jesus, that God is interested
in our simple hunger. Through him, and Jesus means now,
everybody will get enough.

Historically and scientifically there remains one question
to answer. Was the primitive community right?

Did the primitive community rightly understand Jesus when they transferred this borrowed theme to him? We have not many but we have enough words of Jesus recognized as such by all schools to decide whether the primitive community had rightly understood him. This story of ours is not historical but it gives a true picture of Jesus. For this legend has a new and comforting message to give us. For it is not enough that it gives a true picture of Jesus to prove its historicity. The story does not ask us, do you believe that Jesus can multiply loaves? This would be a teaching about Jesus the magician. It asks us, do you trust God to feed you? This is not a teaching *about* Jesus but a living with *Jesus*.

The world view of Jesus' time is no longer operative. Heaven is not above nor hell below, the devil cannot be contacted through frogs' entrails, and sickness is not caused by demons. We no longer think in this way. And we should be careful not to try by means of fantastical constructions to make the biblical stories more probable than they are. For Jesus did not want to perpetuate a world view full of demons, he assumed it quite simply. He wanted to say in its terms why he had come. The job of theology now is not to eliminate the historically untenable and mythical material, but to understand it in terms of our own lives. This process, of which you have just read an example, has an unfortunate name, demythologization, and a happier one, "existential interpretation". The pioneer is the New Testament theologian Rudolf Bultmann. It systematically makes use of the methods of form criticism. It presupposes that theology is not about a particular world view but, may we say it, about God. This would be liable to lead to misunderstanding for it is very easy to tie God to a particular world view.

Doing theology, as we said at the beginning, is to say about God what he does to us. What does God do to us when we hear the legend of the feeding of the five thousand? He makes a promise to us about the starving world. He will not leave this world to itself. Existential interpretation is the attempt to say precisely about God what he does to us, that and nothing more.

4
Theology and the Reunion of the Churches

There is no doubt that one of the major signs of our times is the interest in the reunion of the Churches. A growing awareness of living in one world, fear of Communism, shame at the present grotesque situation, all this may have contributed towards making the question of reunion seem more urgent now and it is, of course, a desire in the spirit of the Gospel.

Christian life is unimaginable without a permanent awareness of this unity. And all Christians today must feel ashamed at the divisions they have made among each other in the name of Jesus Christ. How could it happen that love and truth were separated?

It is easy to ask these questions, but a simple desire for unity solves nothing. No one who is concerned about unity can escape the necessary rigorous theological examination of the concept itself. The work of reunion in this generation and the next will not succeed if unity is only desired and prayed for and no work done. This work for unity is beset with difficulties arising from prejudice, tradition and historical accidents.

I would like to do a little of this work for you now. A book was published in Rome by the young Austrian theologian Hasenhüttl, a dissertation for the Papal Gregorian University. It appeared in a series whose general title was *Koinonia*, that is communion, community. The book is about Protestant theology with which it seeks to engage in dialogue at its best.

A proper partner is not that form of Protestantism which is fixated on the sixteenth century and awaits all its salvation thence, neither is it that form of Protestantism which has given up and turned inwards upon itself, relying upon an easy piety, but precisely that theology which was abused as "destructive", "abstract", "seeking to solve everything" by Catholics and respectable Protestants alike. I mean the theology of Rudolf Bultmann, and this is the partner Hasenhüttl engages in his book. Under the title "The fulfilment of faith" Hasenhüttl attempts "an encounter between Rudolf Bultmann and the Catholic understanding of the faith". The surprising thing about this book is how close this genuinely Catholic thought has been able to come to what might be called an extreme of Protestant theology. In his foreword Bultmann writes that he has seldom found such a clear understanding of his thought as in this book.

For while Protestants often assert that Bultmann is a necessary but already superseded intermediary phase, and while the opposed camps become hardened in their attitudes, or, even worse, softened through their acceptance of a sort of "existential interpretation" which understands everything and criticizes nothing, here the dialogue is taken up as it needs to be, courageously and serenely asking the right questions. The author escapes the prejudices of both left and right and gives us a precise existential-philosophical account of the subject.

Hasenhüttl regards the "fulfilment of faith" as the central issue of Bultmann's theology. My "act of faith" as my allowing-myself-to-be-determined by my encounter with Christ. It is remarkable that this book, which is written with a close familiarity with its sources and seeks to discern the inner movement of Bultmann's theology, leaves the problem of demythologizing right in the background. This illustrates how a certain kind of theological controversy is a betrayal of both truth and love. In a proper dialogue on these matters, a dialogue which seeks understanding and not an easy victory, it appears that Hasenhüttl, without actually saying so, takes demythologizing for granted, it is faith come to maturity. He who believes demythologizes; there is no such thing as faith untranslated. Faith is the acceptance of a doctrine or, better, since these days we have no conception of a doctrine which can demand absolute allegiance, the acceptance of an opinion which is subject to investigation and can be put down on paper. Faith does not come to maturity by being interrogated with questions like "what do you think of Christianity?" or "Do you believe in God?" This leads at the most to an opinion on the existence of a heavenly being. Hasenhüttl is very well aware of all this and it enables him to demonstrate in his book the real benefits of "existential interpretation".

What does "existential" mean? Why is theology so keen on this term which has already gone out of philosophical fashion? Because by it it can guard against two common misunderstandings. First the orthodox doctrinal one which seeks to establish the faith upon objective facts, from Bethlehem to the Ascension, and second the pietistic and subjective which seeks to establish the faith solely upon the believer and his experiences. But faith as a way of life among others is not to be found in the sphere of fact or the sphere of opinion, and anyone who will admit nothing beyond these structures of fact and opinion which look unpleasantly like a crude Marxist base and superstructure, is making an ontological assumption of a vulgarly positivistic kind, an assumption which can be corrected neither by accuracy of dogma nor depth of piety. Theology defends itself against this positivistic ontology, in which even God can only be either a fact or an opinion (and both these conceptions are blasphemous), with the term "existence". It refers to a kind of being which comes to light

neither through objective demonstration nor through subjective
experience but is whatever we feel to be most real in our faith
or our fears, our hope or despair, our loving or our existing
for ourselves alone. These actions can of course be registered
objectively or subjectively, statistical and psychological
research can be done upon them, but this Cartesian approach
misses the very thing we are talking about.

Let us take an example of a problem which has long been
at issue between Catholic and Evangelical, the problem of
human nature.

The reformers, faced with Catholic doctrine on the damage
done to human nature by the Fall, repeatedly asserted "the
thoughts of a man's heart are evil from his youth". The
Council of Trent, however, taught the original integrity of
man. Even after the Fall he is still capable of free choice, he is
not under a physical compulsion to sin, his will is still free
even though man in the concrete "is in no way capable of
truly loving God" (Bellarmine). The Catholic teaching is also
that man cannot attain the grace of God by moral endeavour
or good works. This grace must first free him from the tendency
to sin which actually possesses him. This tendency must not
be regarded as his inevitable fate. He is subject to it in his
actual condition but the tendency has not corrupted his
"nature"; even when he is a sinner he is a being meant for
God, even when he is a sinner his heart is restless and he
seeks salvation. This is the central point of the Catholic teaching. Something in man remains constant, even when he is a
sinner he remains God's creature.

Reformed doctrine, on the other hand, holds that nothing
"good" remains in man, not in the sense that he is actually
incapable of a good action but in the strict sense that this
concrete human being does not want God, he says no to God,
could not of his own accord say yes, because a damaged

relationship between persons cannot be repaired by mere goodwill or the readiness of the offending party to make amends. The offending party has, as it were, lost the right to act, the next move must come from the other side, and in this sense the offending party is not free. This helplessness was given the name "corruption of human nature" in the reformed doctrine, for their terminology derived from the Catholic. It is an unfortunate expression when we consider that it is here used to refer not to man's nature but to his history, his experiences.

Hasenhüttl the Catholic in dialogue with Bultmann the Protestant shows very clearly how this debate about human nature can be settled with the help of a new terminology. Both parties are right, but they are regarding the question from a different angle. Catholic thought is systematic and ontological, the Protestant existential and ontic. Ontologically speaking, man is, as Hasenhüttl says, "ambivalent". To claim that he is unfree and totally corrupted is to deny his personal character which he keeps even when he is a sinner. Ontically speaking, in the existential experience of the sinner this knowledge is of no use to him whatever.

For this ontological freedom, which is expressed for example in despair over his own sins, cannot in fact be regained or put to work by his own efforts. To take a biblical example, when the publican prays, "Lord, be merciful to me a sinner", he knows nothing about his free will and his uncorrupted nature. Luther thought of this publican as the damned, for whom nothing remained but grace. He considered looking beyond one's own personal existence as escape, useless and bringing no comfort. He was thinking existentially.

The Catholic theologians did not think of this story from the point of view of the publican but from the point of view of Christ, who told the story and saw in the publican's despairing prayer the fact that God had given even to him a way out of his situation. The Catholic is thinking ontologically.

In the debate about human nature, the publican must say: "I am bad", the narrator and onlooker must say at this point in the story: "You are at a crisis" or, with Hasenhüttl, "You are ontologically ambivalent". It appears that both sides have overemphasized part of the truth. In fact there is no contradiction between them. And there are many other issues where this would prove to be the case with the help of Bultmann's theology.

Different preoccupations and emphases which express themselves in different language must be clarified. It remains to be seen whether this difference can be overcome or whether it should be kept and a common teaching and a common life of faith can be achieved despite it.

5

Or should we wait for Another?

Advent means arrival. The calendar describes the four Sundays
in the time before Christmas as "Advent" Sundays. Does Jesus
arrive like a train at a railway station? We might think so, the
way Christmas comes in as surely as any express. Does it make
any difference whether there is someone waiting anxiously on
the station? No, Jesus does not come like this. If no one was
waiting for him he would not come, whatever the calendar
said.

But who is waiting for Jesus? I should like to say, everybody. Everyone alive is waiting, and, moreover, everyone is
waiting for Jesus.

Everyone alive is waiting. The more alive he is the more
clearly this appears. John the Baptist was a man who spent his
whole life waiting. Waiting is not passive. Waiting does not
mean sitting still with my hands in my lap and my eyes uplifted.
On the contrary, John wandered about between the wilder-
ness, the Jordan and the capital, and he needed his hands to dip
the multitudes in the cleansing waters, and he could not lift
his eyes up to heaven because he had to look at the people to
whom he had something important to say. He did not wait
in stillness like a flower for the dew. He did not wait, saying
time will tell. He waited impatiently and when the time came
he was not vindicated but killed. This waiting was not easy.
It imposed a particular way of life upon him, a way of life
whose meaning was the "future", "soon", "tomorrow" or

"when he comes". He fasted because he was waiting, he preached because he was waiting, he baptized because he was waiting. He went to prison because he had dared to wait. This shows how dangerous it is to put all your eggs in one basket. A crisis came and John in prison sent messengers to Jesus asking, "Are you the one who is to come or must we wait for another?"

Everyone who has ever had to wait will know that it is impossible without a picture of the absent person. Those who wait in hope imagine the expected person delightfully. In this respect John was not ascetic. He had imagined, as had his fathers, the glorious messianic kingdom. Towards the end of his life—and he was no older than the person he preached—this picture dissolved before his eyes and he had to face the reality. John thought of himself as too little, unworthy, to serve him who was to come. In fact he who was to come had no use for the division of people into worthy and unworthy. John thought he was not worthy to untie his sandal strap, but he who was to come thought it perfectly normal to wash his friends' feet. John spoke of judgment and the final separation of the good and the wicked, but he who was to come did not judge but called people blessed. John saw the new kingdom coming, coming quickly, but Jesus did nothing to fulfil the ancient dream. John's hope became uncertain and his imaginings were confounded.

There were many who like John were prepared to believe in Jesus. All they wanted was his final vindication by God. His mother, his brothers, his disciples all asked the same question as John in prison. "Are you he who is to come or must we wait for another?" Jesus was not what they expected, not what Jewish tradition had expected. Expectation and fulfilment were so unalike that people began to ask, has there been a mistake? Is he really the right person? Or should we wait for another?

The waiting passed into a state of crisis. It became critical, doubting, questioning, but, let us not forget, it was till waiting. The imaginings were damaged, but hope was not damaged; John went on waiting in prison and his messengers did not ask Jesus, "Are you the one or have we waited in vain?" or "Are you the one or should we give up?" This idea which occurs so promptly to us did not enter their heads or anyone else's who was waiting like them. They could not conceive of human life without waiting.

What is important is not what someone is but what he is waiting for. Not the events of life but its possibilities. To know a man is not to know his past, to reveal his essence or describe his set-up, but to define his relation to the future. It makes little sense in biblical terms to say John, who used to baptize and preach, is now in prison. Better to say John is a man who does not cease to wait for the kingdom of God even in prison. In the first account John has nothing more to wait for, the present is described in terms of the past. In the second the present is still defined in terms of the future. The important thing is still to come. I do not mean that John is not yet dead. But that the hope which ruled his whole life is still present in his imprisonment and will also rule his death.

The important thing is still to come, man is a being who can wait. This is something that does not come of its own accord but must be learnt, as we can see from watching young children who find it very hard to understand that "soon", "later" or "tomorrow" do not mean never. When a child learns to wait, he learns to enjoy things more and for a longer time. He has a future. Everyone alive is waiting. This does not mean simply carrying on from day to day. A human being does not pass from today to tomorrow like a stone. He has a relationship to the future and he is afraid or confident.

But there are people, like the people in a poem by Bert

Brecht, who say, "Everything stays the same. Nothing ever turns out as we want it to." Waiting is foolishness, hoping is an illusion which melts away in the sunshine of reality. But can a human being go on living permanently without expecting anything? "Everything stays the same", no one keeps up this attitude, for as the Preacher says, "All living things hope. A living dog is better than a dead lion." Here living is taken as the ability to hope. "Everything remains the same." If we can call anything "atheistic", it is this attitude. But this is not a final condemnation, for God does not abandon those who give him up by denying the future.

Bert Brecht puts these words in the mouth of authority, for it is interested in maintaining the *status quo*. But his answer to those who are resigned to the situation is:

> Let the living never say never.
> What is sure is not sure.
> Things do not stay as they are.

To be content with the world as it is is to be dead. And this includes everybody. Many promises are broken, many wishes remain unfulfilled and many sins unpunished. Waiting begins with saying no, with refusing to accept a second best. This is not it, say those who are waiting. This is not it, says John. This is not it, say all those who have anything to do with Advent. In the *Threepenny Opera*, Jenny the pirate's bride sings a song which is entirely about Advent, like the carol "I saw three ships". It is a different style but we can still learn something from Brecht about waiting:

> Sirs, you see me washing up today,
> I make beds for you all.
> You give me a penny
> and I am grateful.

You see my rags and tatters
and this tatty hotel.
But who it is you're talking to
you never could tell.

For one evening
in the harbour
there will be a cry
for a ship with eight sails
and fifty canon
standing at the quay.

Is not today always tatty like this little kitchen-maid's hotel?
All Advent songs are about what is going to happen one
evening soon; all refuse to be bound by the present. It is
always today and "one evening". If this is interpreted as above
and below, valley of tears and heavenly bliss, this is a misunderstanding of the Christian hope, a diminishment, for God
promises more when he says "soon" than when he says
"above". John at any rate expected more than the reopening
of the gates of heaven; he expected someone to come and
transform this world by his coming.

But in that case hadn't he mistaken the person he was waiting
for and shouldn't he look for another? Even when we agree
that what is important is what we are waiting for and that
everyone alive is waiting, even if we refuse an attitude of
resignation to authority and say, "Things do not stay as they
are, the sure is unsure", is this a reason for putting our hope
in Jesus of Nazareth? What desires has he ever fulfilled?

In fact we are waiting for quite other things, for a wage
increase, a new flat, a holiday or a new friend, that is for the
happiness which comes from many little things. But we need
to make a correction here. Of course Jenny and all we other
kitchen-maids are waiting for the ship with eight sails to carry
us away. But our great hope, which, as Luther says, turns away

from the present and longs for the future, our true Advent, is not concerned with our little hopes of private happiness. Understandable though it may be, it is in the long run quite impossible to hope only for private happiness. Even on one's private little island of delight, the cries of the oppressed cannot be stifled. The needs of others still reach us. The desire for an island happiness in this sea of troubles is not a large enough desire.

While we are waiting we picture what we want to come. We need someone to heal our ills, take care of us, ease our difficulties and dispel our boredom. Jesus does not do this. If we must have this, we should look for another. If, however, we begin to wait for God, we must first suffer the experience of John, the type of all waiting men, that God destroys the imaginings of our expectations. To wait for God means to let the future we wanted fall away and yet go on waiting.

Jesus' answer to him who was awaiting the kingdom of righteousness and peace is very remarkable. Jesus says that this kingdom, about which all one can say is that God is near, is already present. He describes it in detail: "The blind see, the lame walk, lepers are cleansed, the deaf hear, the dead are raised and the poor have the gospel preached to them."

And after this description of the kingdom, which takes up the words of the prophet Isaiah but transfers them from the future to the present, Jesus adds, "Blessed is he who does not lose confidence in me". This is very puzzling, for if John had waited aright and Jesus confirmed all that he had hoped for, what reason could he have for losing confidence in him? Why should a hope that had been fulfilled, and hope is always hope against sickness, suffering and death, find a reason to lose confidence and be disappointed? But Jesus expects just this disappointment. The most natural and probable course would be to look for another. Does Jesus really fulfil the expectation of John? Is God already present? Is there peace in the world? Have we waited long enough?

We can only answer this question in a contradictory way. The answer is yes *and* no. Yes, Jesus says, God is with you. The kingdom is in the midst of you. You need not think that you have longed for it too long. The poor have the Gospel preached to them. That is to say, those who have waited so long are now told, He for whom you waited has come. The time has come. You did not ask too much when you wanted to be loved. All those who waited have a reason to rejoice.

But behind the Christmas tree we already see the shadows of the cross. Behind the yes there is a no. "Blessed is he who does not lose confidence in me." To tell the truth I cannot understand anyone who does *not* lose confidence in Jesus. To begin with, "the blind see, the lame walk . . ." The blind I know grope painfully through the world and the lame are in wheel-chairs. Should it be taken less literally? But what can one take literally, that is to say seriously, if not Jesus? Of course he healed a few, and some of the blind in the time of Jesus recovered their sight, but what does "the blind see" mean when so many remain who have not recovered their sight? Did not lepers die in Jerusalem when Jesus was in Capernaum? No, the miracles of Jesus are perhaps an indication that God means well by us, but they are not a proof of his friendship. If there are Christians who can console themselves for God not caring about Ausschwitz by remembering a few of the miracles and sayings of Jesus, this sounds to me like the heedless faith which can indeed move mountains—and such mountains of suffering and misery—but this, according to the apostle Paul, profits them nothing because they lack the one thing necessary.

But Jesus knew all this. He did not say simply, Yes, you have waited long enough and now everything is all right. He also said, No, you must still go on waiting. You must still wait for him who is already present. He is present but you must go on waiting for him sounds absurd. But it is an exact description of the Christian life. God is present but how? He is invisible, incalculable and as rare as true love.

Love is incalculable. Every action is subject to many interpretations. Was it done for love, for profit, for fame, or out of fear? Love, including the love of God, does not prove itself by a few actions visible to any observer. Where there is real love—and who is to say that the incalculable is unreal?—there must be someone receiving it who believes in it. Jesus does not take away God's invisibility. He says plainly, God is present, but he says it meaning that we can, perhaps, believe in him but not photograph him. "Giving sight to the blind and raising the dead are small matters compared to the preaching of the Gospel to the poor." So Luther says of Jesus who preaches the invisible God. If God is present but invisible, this is a reason either to lose confidence or to go on waiting.

Waiting does not stop because love remains unrevealed. The present and the future are engaged in a tension which must seem absurd to the materialist eye. For either something is present or I wait for it, either I have something or I don't have it. But relations between people conceived entirely in terms of possessing or not possessing are very corrupt. In marriage, for example, the partner is there, present, and you must wait for each other, future. When this expectation becomes less and less and is replaced by possession, then the past begins to take over the future. The couple know each other, they expect nothing new. Only hope keeps us alive, hope of the unknown.

It is therefore necessary to retain the contradiction between the present and the future and not to seek a one-sided solution. There is in John's impatience the danger that the present will be betrayed by the future. From the "this is not it" in the world of the tatty hotel, there grows a picture of the only proper situation which is impatient of the imperfect and to which the present, however tatty, is sacrificed. This form of hope, of which crude Marxism is the clearest example, is not really waiting for the future but for a predetermined picture which makes allowances for nothing else. To wait in this way is to wait only for oneself.

The other false solution is to betray the future in the name of the present, the capitalist error. We call our tatty world a perfectly pleasant place, make no plans for future improvements, think five years ahead at most, if possible enlist Jesus in our schema, and give up waiting because the one thing we care about is already there, ourselves.

Everyone who waits, waits for Jesus. This means all who are really waiting do not only wait for bliss above or their own private happiness. All who really wait do not wait for themselves, for their picture of the future, but for something new, for what we called the revelation of God. All who wait, wait for God's kingdom, as Jesus did for the kingdom which is already present. Waiting for Jesus, then, means waiting like Jesus.

The tension between present and future remains unrelaxed, for to be a Christian means to be in an Advent situation not just for four Sundays. Because God loves our tatty present there is hope for the future. Only because the one we waited for is already present can we go on waiting for him. Advent tells us to wait. "Blessed are the homesick." This is how Jung-Stilling describes the Christian. Meaning not that you will be blessed when you no longer need to wait but now in your homesickness, here in exile awaiting the revelation of God, you are blessed. You do not lose confidence because God is invisible, you do not forget that you live by hope and not possession, and you go on waiting. This not incidentally, or occasionally, but in all you do, think and are. Such an attitude which determines a whole life cannot endure if the picture of what is awaited is made absolute or forced to express our whole expectation. God is greater than our heart, which does not mean that we should give up the desires of our heart, our dreams and our hopes of him. But the fulfilment of our hope is beyond its vision and our future is beyond our expectation.

Should we wait for another, who will give us back our health or Germany her unity? Or should we wait for God? This does not mean to pray for the future whatever it may be, this would be a belief in blind fate and not the living God, who is the ground of our hope in the transformation of the world. How could we not form a picture of a better world to come, when this world is given into our hands and we are responsible for it? But this picture is not the only measure, for God is greater than our heart.

We must wait with concrete plans and hopes, private and public, but we must subject them to the correction of God. Christian waiting is to imagine the future but to be ready to renounce our imaginings. This is only possible if we believe that God is already present. God is already present in the coming of Jesus of Nazareth who gave us the future. Because God came into the world unknown we are waiting for his revelation, for his kingdom which is already present and to come. Should we wait for another, who speaks more plainly and leaves a better world behind him? Or should we begin to wait for God?

6

Why do you seek the Living among the Dead?

THE EMPTY TOMB AND MODERN THEOLOGY

A conversation

(*A: Orthodox; B: Liberal; C: Documentation*)

C: To think for oneself means to make oneself, that is one's own reason, the final arbiter of the truth. The maxim, always to think for oneself, is enlightenment. (Kant)

B: Readers of the *Berlinische Monatsschrift* for October 1786 who read Kant's paper: "What does directing my own thoughts mean?" were addressed as *adult* people.

C: If we were to ask, Are we now living in an enlightened epoch? the answer would be no, but we live in an epoch of *enlightenment*. As things are, we have still a long way to go before most people are capable of following their own understanding in religious matters without being directed by others. (Kant)

B: Is this work begun in the eighteenth century *now* completed? I don't think so, at least in religious matters. Or in the last two hundred years have Christians put away their childish ways?

A: Quite a lot of work in this direction has been done, for example the emancipation of the laity. I am thinking of the much publicized talk of the secular world which must presuppose an adult Christian.

B: The *word* "adult" is often used, but one cannot feel much confidence in it so long as Christians keep the same reservations about the word "enlightenment" as at the time when Lessing published the *Fragments of Biblical Criticism of the unknown Hermann Samuel Reimarus.* For Kant the adult state, which does not come of itself but with the arrival of a certain age, implies enlightenment and a refusal to reserve certain spheres from rational investigation. Anyone who takes the risk of thinking for himself, of being adult, cannot reserve the Easter story for pious assent.

A: Enlightenment concerning the Bible means to treat the texts of Matthew, Mark, Luke or John in the same way as texts of Herodotus or Thucydides. But has the time yet come for this enterprise which many Christians might find disturbing?

B: Let Lessing answer you:

C: My unknown friend—I do not know when he wrote— believed that the times must first become more enlightened before he could preach what he held to be true. I believe that before the times can become more enlightened we must first investigate whether what he held to be true really is so. With all due praise to the sobriety and caution of my unknown friend, I wish he had shown less confidence in his proofs, less contempt for the common man and less distrust of his own times.

B: The Church has declared for too long that the time is not yet ready and thereby left the progress of the enlightenment to the non-Christians who have pursued it more single-mindedly and with more success.

C: The destruction of religion as the illusory happiness of the people is to demand their real happiness. The demand to give up illusions is a demand to give up a condition which *requires* illusions. The critique of religion is therefore the critique of the valley of tears glorified by religion. *Religion is the opium of the people.* (Karl Marx)

B: Whenever Christianity and enlightenment appear to be contradictory, then Marx is correct.

A: But there are childish minds which are unmoved by the insights and problems of scientific criticism. Is their religion opium? And is it right to disturb or even destroy this faith through historical criticism?

B: But there are also minds created by God who cannot ignore the criticisms. Lessing, again, pointed out the severest criticisms of the resurrection accounts, even though these criticisms did not convince him.

C: Those of my readers who do not question their religion are more fearful than well instructed. They may be very *pious* Christians but they are certainly not very *enlightened* Christians. They may have very good intentions towards their religion but they should have more confidence in it. (Lessing)

B: The enlightened Christian, that is to say the adult Christian, is not afraid of the historical critical scrutiny of the Bible. Because adulthood is no longer the privilege of the few we can no longer bypass the historical question, what really happened at Easter?

A: Can the historian answer it?

B: He must try.

C: A flame needs a draught to blow it out. (Lessing)

B: This is what Lessing wrote. This is what he did. His opponents, the orthodox, "a squinting, limping orthodoxy at odds with itself", did all they could to put out the fire. They tried to harmonize the contradictions in the evangelists' accounts which the unknown Reimarus pointed out.

A: Lessing, on the contrary, did something very silly which one of his opponents recorded to sneer at.

C: Before the Lord Mayor of London stands a man accused of arson. He was seen coming out of the burning house. "Yesterday at four o'clock," he says, "I came upon my neighbour's barn and found in it a burning torch which the servants had carelessly left. It would have burnt down in the night and caught the staircase on fire. I threw straw on it so that the flames reached the window and the firemen came as fast as they could to put it out. So the fire was extinguished, but if it had been left to burn all night it would have become dangerous." "Why did you not simply take the torch and put it out?" asked the Lord Mayor. "If I had put out the torch the servants would not have become more careful. Now that there has been such a fuss they will take great care in future." "Amazing," said the Lord Mayor. "He is not really a bad man, only not quite right in the head." And he sent him to the madhouse and there he remains till this day.

B: The story suits Lessing. But he was not mad, he knew what he was doing. Albert Schweitzer writes about Reimarus:

C: It was the first time that a historically minded person, who was well acquainted with the sources, undertook the criticism of the tradition. The language is concise and dry, epigrammatic, as befits a man in search of facts rather than a fine style. Occasionally, however, it reaches heights of true emotion, like mysterious pictures painted by a Vulcan's fire on dark clouds. There has seldom been so fierce a hatred and so fine a contempt. There has seldom been a work written with such absolute superiority of insight over its contemporaries. Lessing's greatness lay in his realization that this criticism was bound to lead either to the destruction *or* the development of the concept of revelation. (A. Schweitzer)

B: This is Reimarus' major thesis:

C: The Easter accounts are a mass of irreconcilable contradictions, which no art in the world could harmonize. No honest and careful reader can trust the Gospel stories. They contradict each other in everything, people, time, place, manner, viewpoint, language and events.

B: Let us hear the witnesses. *Who* came to the tomb on Easter morning?

C: According to Mark it was the three women, Mary Magdalene, Mary the mother of James, and Salome. According to Matthew it was two women. According to Luke it was three women mentioned by name and others, that is to say at least five. According to John it was Mary Magdalene alone.

B: It was one, two, three or at least five women who claimed to have seen the empty tomb. Furthermore, when did they come, at sunrise or while it was still dark, as John says?

C: According to Mark and Luke they wanted to anoint the body.

B: The very idea is not merely unusual but impossible. To anoint a body after it has lain in the grave a day and two nights, and that in the climate of Palestine. And the burial itself did not take place in haste or disorder.

C: Therefore Matthew amended that the women came to look at the grave.

B: What did they see?

C: According to Mark, Luke and John, they saw that the stone had been moved away, but according to Matthew they saw an angel from heaven, who moved the stone away from the entrance to the tomb.

B: Whom did they see?

C: According to Mark and Matthew they saw an angel, according to Luke and John, they saw two angels who told them that Jesus had risen from the dead.

B: What did the women do when they received the good news?

C: According to Mark they kept silence and were afraid, according to Matthew they told with great joy what they had seen, according to Luke they told their news but no one believed them.

B: It follows that none of these stories agree with each other. Some even contain internal contradictions.

C: For example, Matthew says that the guards of the grave fainted with fright when they saw the angel come down from heaven and move the stone, but nevertheless they later gave an account of it all and not, as one would expect of soldiers, to the Roman superiors, but directly to the high priests. The high priests bribed them with a lot of money not merely to keep quiet but to spread abroad the lie that the body had been stolen by the disciples while they, the soldiers, were asleep.

B: This story is so improbable, factually, logically and psychologically that it is irredeemable, a later legend.

A: Granted this may be so, the question remains in whose interest was it to invent it. May not its very improbability be evidence of its historicity? There can have been little point in inventing something so improbable.

B: But we know exactly what interest was behind the invention of this legend. It was not idle fantasy but self-defence. The Easter stories were regarded by the Jewish and Gentile world as the products of fantasy, fairy stories, women's gossip.

C: Three objections to the story are made in the New Testament itself. According to Matthew, the high priests came to Pilate and said, "Command the grave to be guarded until the third day so that his disciples cannot come and steal the body and tell the people he has risen from the

dead". Luke relates of the disciples: They were terrified
and thought they were seeing a ghost.

B: Is this a refined form of deception or crude superstition on
the part of the disciples? But they managed to deal with
this objection. The third is an even more difficult one, first
formulated by Celsus in the second century and taken up by
Reimarus and many others.

C: Christ should have appeared to his enemies if the resurrection was a reality.

A: This is also mentioned in the New Testament.

C: In the Acts of the Apostles Peter says: Him God has
raised up and manifested, not to all the people but to *us*,
the predestined witnesses of God, who ate and drank with
him after he rose from the dead.

B: Matthew, however, tries to come to grips with the opponents of the new Christendom and seeks neutral witnesses
in the guards. The other point in his account is also late
and legendary, that the resurrection itself was witnessed,
and the other evangelists avoid this. They keep the secret
of the resurrection and say only that the grave was empty.

A: The so-called apocryphal gospels, on the other hand,
describe in detail how Jesus visibly rose from the grave
and went up to heaven. The gospel of Peter has the scribes,
the Pharisees and the elders go to Pilate and demand a
guard for three days. They get soldiers with a named
commander, Petronius, and, as in Matthew, go with them
to the grave and seal it with seven seals. The crowds from
Jerusalem and the surrounding country come too to see
the sealing of the grave. Then they drift away, but the
elders remain there the following night with the soldiers,
who had put up a tent by the grave, and they are eye-
witnesses of the resurrection.

C: In the night before the Lord's day, as the soldiers were

D

keeping watch in pairs, a mighty sound came from heaven
and they saw the heavens open and two men in rich apparel
come down and approach the grave. The stone which was
at the door of the grave rolled away of its own accord and
the grave was opened and the two young men went in.
When the soldiers saw it, they woke up the centurion and
the elders, for they too were keeping watch. And while
they were still telling what they had seen they saw three
men coming out of the grave, the two who had gone in
leading a third, and a cross came behind them, and the
head of the two that led the third man reached up to
heaven and the head of the third man reached beyond
heaven. And a voice came out of heaven: "Have you
preached to the sleepers?" And from the cross came the
answer, "Yes". Then the witnesses decided to go and tell
Pilate. (Gospel of Peter)

B: There is no need to criticize the apocryphal fantasy, in
which heathen soldiers see the risen Lord and recognize
him before Jesus appears to his friends, and in which his
enemies are the witnesses of his resurrection. But these
tendencies are already present in Matthew.

A: Which is the very reason why the earlier Gospel accounts
sound genuine in their restraint and severity. They do
indeed contradict each other in nearly every detail, but
this itself gives the historian confidence that they did not
copy each other and that they are all the more likely to be
independent and very old traditions.

B: They *could* be. Accounts which agreed in every detail would
be suspect, but this does not make accounts which disagree
respectable.

A: Nevertheless, one should not fall into complete scepticism,
which even Lessing avoids, and one should ask what they do
agree about. For the accounts do have something in common.

B: The basic schema is this: the grave was found empty by the women. Christ appeared to his disciples and after forty days went up to heaven. But as far as the stories go, we know nothing for certain about what time he spent with his disciples.

A: But the witnesses are not writing history. They are preaching in stories and not giving information about historical facts. They want to force their hearers to make a decision.

B: We agree on this. The gospels are not historical documents. But we disagree on what facts are the basis for their preaching.

A: On a careful analysis we can distinguish two separate groups.

C: The accounts of the empty tomb might be called negative resurrection accounts. Originally they were only about women followers of Jesus and not the disciples. Christ does not appear in them, only the angel. The accounts of the appearances of Jesus, on the other hand, are not originally connected with the empty tomb. They are about the disciples, not the women. In them there are no angels but the Lord himself appears.

B: This gives rise to one of the most difficult problems. *Where* did Christ appear to his disciples?

C: According to Luke's gospel and Acts the appearances all happened in and around Jerusalem, according to John likewise (except in his later additional chapter). According to Matthew and Mark the appearances happened in Galilee.

A: Does this really matter? Christ can appear to his disciples wherever he likes.

B: Certainly, but the historian wants to know where the disciples were when they saw him. For one cannot judge the truth of the story until one has got the details straight.

A: But on this point isn't it quite easy to reconcile the Mark and Matthew Galilee accounts and the Luke and John accounts of Jerusalem?

B: But the question where he first appeared remains unanswered. *Either* Christ appeared first to his disciples in Jerusalem, and only then in Galilee, or not.

C: Luke and John know nothing of further appearances in Galilee.

B: But then one would need to explain what made the disciples go up to Galilee and then come back to Jerusalem. In this case the belief in the resurrection is dependent on the empty tomb. *Or*, as a number of critics maintain, the first appearances took place in Galilee independently of the empty tomb.

A: Is there therefore no point in asking where were the disciples on Easter day? They were in Jerusalem.

B: This is precisely what is in question.

C: Mark and Matthew both agree that when Jesus was arrested all the disciples fled. Even Peter only dares to follow Jesus from afar and then abandons him. From then on the three oldest evangelists agree that no disciples remained with Jesus either when he was carrying his cross or when he was crucified. Only women who had followed him from Galilee, looked on "from afar". None of the evangelists relates whether any one of the disciples was present at the burial of Jesus. This explains why, after the execution of Jesus, no effort was made to get the disciples, it was clearly not worth the bother.

B: We may assume that the disciples had fled home from Jerusalem to Galilee. Where else would they go? They would become fishermen again. The Gospel of Peter also tells this story.

C: "It was the last day of the unleavened bread, and many

were leaving and going home because the feast was over. But we, the twelve disciples of the Lord, wept and were full of sorrow. And each went to his own house, grieving over what had happened. I, Simon Peter, and my brother Andrew took our nets and went out on the lake." (Gospel of Peter)

B: The disappointed and hopeless disciples saw the risen Lord in Galilee, and they only went back to Jerusalem because they believed in him.

A: Granted that a simple solution to the question of place is not to be had, what facts remain ascertainable to the historian?

B: The risen Lord meets Peter and then the twelve in Galilee, this is confirmed by Paul, Galilee where they had fled. At this meeting they are sent back to Jerusalem with a mission to preach the message of the risen Lord. There are further appearances to the growing community. The legend of the empty tomb grows up later.

A: I do not agree. The empty tomb story, even though it has acquired legendary accretions, is well attested by all the evangelists; and secondly, it does not necessarily contradict the accounts of the resurrection appearances in Galilee and Jerusalem.

B: This is a serious difficulty and the best thing to do is to call the most important witness, the apostle Paul.

C: His account fulfils all the conditions for historical reliability. It is exact and concise, and is in fact simply a list of appearances. "First to Cephas, then to the twelve, then he appeared to more than five hundred brethren at once, most of whom are still alive. . . ."

A: In other words their witness is still verifiable.

C: "but some have fallen asleep. Then he appeared to James, and then to all the apostles. Last of all, he appeared to me as to one who was born out of due time." Paul stresses that he is only passing on the message he has received. 1 Corinthians in which the passage occurs, was written in 56 or 57, that is about twenty-five years after the death of Jesus. Paul probably received this traditional formula shortly after his conversion in 33 or 35. This brings us very close to the Easter event. At the very latest this formula dates from ten years after the crucifixion, probably earlier, whereas the earliest gospel, Mark, was not written until the year 70.

A: The resurrection is not concerned with the spiriting away of a heavenly being, such as featured in cultic liturgies of the time, but with an event which at least in its effects is verifiable.

B: But Paul's schema is not the one we mentioned earlier. The Gospel schema was empty tomb, appearances, resurrection. Paul's is resurrection, scriptural proof, appearances.

A: This is not necessarily contradictory. The question is how does our oldest and most reliable account, that of Paul, tally with the gospels?

B: If we begin with what is undisputed, the appearances to the disciples, first in Galilee and then in Jerusalem, Paul is with us. But as he numbers his own encounter with Christ on the road to Damascus among these appearances, some of which are documented in the gospels, we are able to say something about them.

C: We can be certain that he who appears is the man Jesus. But he who speaks to Paul has a ghostly body. He does not walk upon the earth but comes from heaven in a mysterious light. The appearances are accompanied by the spoken word, whose purpose is to give a mission.

B: They appear not to be heard or seen by all who are present, but only by those whom they concern, that is to say those who through them learn to believe. There is therefore no reason against describing these appearances as "visions", if that is how one describes the occurrence on the road to Damascus.

A: Vision? Does this mean an "illusion" that corresponds to no reality?

B: No reality that can be photographed at any rate. To *whom* did he actually appear? Celsus in his time sneered at people who wanted to prove the resurrection by means of the appearances.

C: Reimarus maintains that the evangelical accounts only agree on one point. Only close followers of Jesus, who were already connected with the circle of apostles, saw the risen Lord. There were no unprejudiced witnesses.

A: But it is historically impossible to discount the appearances as the products of fantasy. For one thing Christ appeared to numerous witnesses over at least three years.

B: This could easily be a psychological chain reaction.

A: But it is of primary importance to remember that he appeared not only to believers, but also to unbelievers, the disappointed, the despairing and even to persecutors like Paul. The appearances do not presuppose faith but arouse it.

B: I agree that it is psychologically inexplicable that the despairing disciples should have turned into witnesses to the faith and martyrs unless *something* happened to them. It cannot be simple wish-fulfilment, for the disciples had given up all hope. It was all up with them.

A: This surely shows that an inner experience would not have been enough. An external event must have taken place. This is where the historian finds a gap. If he is honest he can either say he doesn't know how after the Golgotha fiasco the faith took root in spite of every natural expectation; or he can accept that something happened that could not have been photographed but is nevertheless a reality. It is not honest to make out that people imagined something: what happened was something unforeseeable and inexplicable. The Christian historian would say that God acted.

B: This would prove our first point, the appearance of the risen Lord, attested by Paul. But on the second point, the empty tomb, he has nothing to say.

A: Because he takes it for granted.

B: I think it is because it does not interest him. He can conceive of the resurrection as a reality *without* the empty tomb. Jesus is not a dead person revivified. Faith in him is not dependent on the empty tomb. Paul at any rate does not consider it necessary to record this doubtful fact in order to believe in the resurrection.

A: But if this evidence in support of faith is well attested, why should we deprive ourselves of it?

B: In the first place the attestation is doubtful, and even if we accept it, how does it help? Apart from the deception hypothesis, what does the return of a dead person to this world prove? It is simply a theme common to many myths.

A: But the appearances do not constitute a proof either. As Lessing says:

C: Religion is not true because the evangelists and the apostles taught it. The evangelists and apostles taught it because it is true. The scriptural traditions must be examined on their internal credibility and all scriptural traditions together could not give religion any internal credibility if it lacked it.

B: With regard to our problem, that is to say that we must give up the theory of inspiration. No historical proof could conjure up the faith or its internal credibility.

A: But I am interested in the corporality, the objectivity of the event. Not imaginings, not visions . . .

B: But still not objective facts. The resurrection of Christ is not a neutral object of observation. The theology of the empty tomb is trying to smuggle in a cameraman and a reporter to record the events of Easter morning, whereas the New Testament thinks only in terms of believers and unbelievers. Those first witnesses had to believe no less than later Christians. There was no wonderful way by which things were made easier for them. It would be a travesty if those who preached belief were themselves dispensed from believing by virtue of what they had seen.

A: But it is not a purely subjective thing either, we cannot reduce it to the psychic experiences of a few ecstatic individuals. The resurrection cannot be historically proved, that is to say "seen", or disproved. All the data are ambivalent. The empty grave could be explained away as deception and the appearances as mere visions. Both historical data can guard the historian against coming to overhasty conclusions. He must at least admit the enormous difficulty of a so-called immanent explanation.

B: On the other hand the historical data can guard the theologian against reaching an overhasty certainty, against calling faith knowledge and the invisible visible. We *know* that the crucifixion happened, but we do not know that the resurrection did. A Catholic theologian has written that it is a question of objective visions willed by God.

A: This is a plausible attempt at harmonizing our two positions. We do not want a theology of the empty tomb or a theology of the pious mind, but a theology of the resurrection.

B: "Why do you seek the living among the dead?" I do not regard these words of the angel as historical but they are the most appropriate to the situation. The women are looking for what they do not and cannot find. For Jesus does not let us find him like a corpse. It is always *he* who finds us. To seek for the living among the dead means to stare into the empty tomb and demand a miracle.

C: The miracles done by Jesus and his disciples were the scaffolding and not the building. (Lessing)

B: The empty tomb and the appearances are miracles in New Testament language, that is to say signs of something else. They are the scaffolding for the building of faith.

A: He who simply stares at the scaffolding is caught in *fides historica*, historical faith, which Luther castigates as false in all his Easter sermons.

C: For most people regard the resurrection of Christ as any other historical event . . . and make it like a picture painted on a wall. (Luther)

A: In this sense, that is the historical, the resurrection of Christ would be an event that concerned him *pro persona sua* but did not concern us.

B: It was Luther who pointed out in the texts that before the appearances of the risen Lord, before the visible signs, stands the invisible word, the angel's message.

C: The risen Christ did not want to appear to anyone before, *ante omnia*, he was announced by word of mouth. Before anything happened without words the angel came from heaven to announce him. Let no one imagine he can grasp Christ except through the word. (Luther)

B: The appearances, therefore, belong to the scaffolding. They are to help the community of the disciples to live by faith, the faith which lives by the word which builds the building Lessing speaks of.

C: The miracles done by Christ and his disciples were the scaffolding and not the building. As soon as the building is finished, the scaffolding is torn away. He whose pride rested in the excellence of the scaffolding, now torn down, would not be interested in the building, for he had been taught that the scaffolding must have had as great a master as the building. Which may well be true. But I am not prepared to bet on it. And I will not let this opinion of the scaffolding prevent me from examining the quality of the building itself. (Lessing)

A: What is the result of this examination of the building?

B: Let Lessing answer for me:

C: A certain subjection of the reason to the obedience of faith is the result of the essential nature of the concept of revelation. Or rather, since the word subjection suggests the exercise of force on the one hand and resistance on the other, the reason *subjects* itself, it admits its own limits, as soon as it is assured of the reality of the revelation. (Lessing)

A: But *when* does reason confess its limits?

B: Not in the examination of historical material! Here it can only reach the as yet undiscovered. If it is forced to confess its limits here, it is only with impatience and not permanently. One should not say:

C: I believe that Jesus Christ was born, died and rose from the dead. But I believe *in* Jesus Christ, who was born, died and rose from the dead.

A: Can this be translated that the limits of reason, which reason itself admits, are visible?

B: I believe in the crucified Lord who is alive, the failure which didn't fail, the defenceless man whom God did not forsake, the man who loved, with whose cause God identified himself.

A: God says yes to what we usually, with good reason, deny. God makes him the lifebringer, whom we thought of as lost in unreality.

B: The reason proves itself enlightened by subjecting itself, admitting its limits, which are the limits of human self-affirmation.

A: God did not arm the defenceless man, he did not let him come to grief, as reason would suppose, but he approved of his defencelessness, accepted and loved him and raised him up. To believe in him means simply to follow his way.

B: He who seeks him among the dead, accepts as true something that happened to him or seeks him among those who are not yet dead, ourselves. He who seeks him among the living, seeks him with God and therefore on this our earth.

7
Against Reason's Despair

The word ghost (German *Geist*, Old and Middle High German *geist*, Old Saxon *gest*) is connected with the ancient Nordic *geisa*, meaning to storm, and the Gothic *usgaisjan*, meaning to bring something out of oneself. It is possible that the ancient Indian words for anger and be angry go back to the same root.

The basic meaning of the German *Geist* (and English ghost) is therefore determined as "being in a state of excitement"—an odd notion upon which one might well reflect. Should we then sing in church "Come, holy excitement"? In fact this hymn is very appropriate to Whitsun. But first allow me a little more linguistics, the purpose of which is to clarify the biblical concept of spirit.

The Hebrew word for spirit or ghost is *ruach*. This is the breath, but not merely the breath of life with which God breathes upon Adam, but the wind which has the power to move man, to drive him, overcome him and carry him away, a power which falls or springs upon him and makes him capable of words and deeds far beyond his normal capabilities. The characteristics of the spirit are spontaneity, it comes unexpectedly, and particularity, that is to say it is linked to a particular time, place and situation and does not act in the same way all the time. The symbol of the wind which blows where it will brings us to the New Testament. The early Church could have made use of the classical Greek word *nous*, the timeless truth embodied in the symbol of unchanging light. But it did not do so and chose a far less likely word, the word *pneuma*, which originally meant no more than breath or wind but came to be used for the life-creating and life-giving breath signified by the Old Testament *ruach*. In neo-Platonic language the *nous* is the highest part of a man within the trichotomy of body, soul, and spirit. In pre-Christian Greek the *pneuma* signifies the un- or the half-conscious. Shocking though it might sound to a Greek ear, the early Christians then proceeded to qualify their chosen word *pneuma* with the adjective holy, a qualification which belonged supremely to the *nous*. This usage thus curiously connects presence to the senses, passion and movement with God, who becomes no longer extra-temporal but the one who empties himself, and whose movement and activity is experienced. It is not the *nous* which is called holy, but the *pneuma*, not clarity but the rushing wind, not light serene but fire.

To understand this would be to follow the movement of the Holy Spirit. This is our only possible means of approach to an idea which is indeed traditional but nevertheless so totally strange as the Holy Spirit. We cannot ask the question, what is the Holy Spirit?—a Greek sort of question—but only the biblical question, what does the Holy Spirit do? What does he bring about? What does he change? We cannot consider the Holy Spirit in terms of his essence, only in terms of his action. We can and should say about the Holy Spirit what he does to us. This is *all* we can say, but we can say this quite clearly.

Unlike the other Christian festivals, Whitsun has never been celebrated with Christmas trees and decorations, little rabbits and eggs. It is a less immediately comprehensible, a more intellectual occasion, more abstract and demanding more reflection, a demand which cannot simply be ignored. I do not think the Holy Spirit has anything to fear from critical reflection and it seems a curious mistake of the times to imagine that his chief enemies are the intellectuals.

Let us consider for a moment the traditional symbol. In the Whitsun story, a rushing mighty wind fills the house, tongues of fire come from heaven, and some fishermen who had been without courage begin to preach and in such a manner that they are heard in many languages at once. Wind, fire and a universal language leave nothing to be desired. A real passion is in question, the spirit and courage to go out and give themselves without fear or reserve. And this passion is ascribed to the working of the Holy Spirit. Mighty wind, fire, universal language: the Holy Spirit does not believe in understatement or he might have come in a little breeze fit only to dry the washing, a small and useful fire and a correct and customary language. But he did not. The Whitsun hymns do not stint their language when they speak about him; they speak of fire burning and glowing.

This passion, in both senses of the word, this enormous excitement, is the work of the Spirit. John's gospel has two expressions for it: (1) The Holy Spirit comforts; (2) he leads to the truth. We should not concentrate on the comfort at the expense of the truth. They belong together. There is no comfort without truth. The Spirit is not a comfortable substitute for him who spent too short a time on earth. This is not comfort. The Spirit comforts *by* leading us to the truth, not by setting it aside. He who does not cling to the truth needs no consolation; he is inconsolable.

Luther says of the Holy Spirit that he is *non scepticus*, he is not a sceptic. This does not mean that the power of the Spirit takes away our power of reflection, criticism and understanding.

The phrase refers rather to a particular attitude to the truth, which with Hegel we may call "the courage to want the truth". It is a measure of the spiritual corruption of our Church life and the stagnation of our spiritual life, that we are respected if we hope for comfort, but the courage to want the truth gets nothing but a wry smile. This is reason's despair. Hegel wrote nearly a hundred and fifty years ago: "You have come as far as Pilate the Roman proconsul. When Christ spoke the word truth he replied with the question, what is truth? in the sense that he was a man who had done with such a word and knew knowledge of the truth to be an impossibility. So what has always been regarded as the most contemptible attitude, the renunciation of the search for truth, has been acclaimed in our time as the highest triumph of the spirit." Perhaps our despair of reason is even greater than that criticized by Hegel. We honour Pilate, the sceptic. Whatever the truth may be, we do not know it and should not even want to. The important thing is to come through, to be a respectable person, to live with our conflicts, and accept the inevitable. It is a great thing to endure the darkness in which we live and he who makes shrill demands for more is beyond our aid. There are grand versions of Pilate discipleship, right down to Gottfried Benn, and this attitude has some very pleasant characteristics; tolerance and understanding friendliness, for example, are both children of scepticism. But the Holy Spirit, God's excitement for the truth, has nothing whatever to do with it. He signals the end of a weary half-certainty, the end of private support, the end of pious sadness. God is excited by the truth. The sin of our time against the Holy Spirit is resignation.

It determines the thought and life structures of a post-revolutionary era. It is the one living religion. A half commitment, a knowledge which foresees that this enthusiasm, this hope, like any other, is liable to come to nothing. It is against all passions, all excitement. The ancient meaning of spirit is meaningless to it. In its despair of reason everything that the Spirit stands for is lost, spontaneity, particularity, passion and the courage to want the truth. In this weariness, the Spirit is not denied, but merely taken to be powerless. He is not to be trusted in the world. Forget that the Spirit can act, lead and work. But the Whitsun story wants us to believe in his power. God is excited by the truth of his cause in the world. There is no reason why this excitement should be left to him alone.

E

8

The Word and Words

Faust in his study trying to translate the prologue to the gospel of John, gets stuck at the first sentence. "In the beginning was the word." He treats it with the distrust of a modern man. "I cannot rate the word so high", and Mephisto mockingly continues: "For when ideas fail, a word comes to the rescue. Words are good for a fight, good for system building, good for exacting faith. . . ."

The word system he is mocking is of course theology, that science which gives the word priority over meaning, power or deed, the substitutes for "Word" that Faust would prefer to put "in the beginning". Faust's reservations stem from the common and deep-rooted feeling that comes out in expressions like "empty words", "mere talk", "manner of speaking".

This distrust of speech has a philosophical background which we can clarify. It is in a philosophical tradition which philosophy and theology today are both at pains to correct. It is not an accident that for both disciplines the problem of language has a sudden new importance. There are congresses, courses of lectures and many new publications on the subject. Philosophy, with the help of sociology, history and logic, has taken up language as an important and largely unexplored problem. And theology, which sees itself as the "language school of faith", is rethinking its basic problems in terms of this new interest in language, and trying to elucidate the word of God by a more advanced knowledge of the nature of human speech. It asks what it means to say that a man hears and obeys, responds and is responsible, understands and interprets, and what all this has to do with the word of God.

What is the cause of this new interest in language? I mean the discriminating kind! For both the word of God and human speech are attacked and misused, misunderstood and abused. Words are thought of as "empty", mere words. This is a situation in which theology and the philosophy of language could be useful to each other. The purpose of this chapter is to seek some sort of dialogue between them, so that theology can profit from the philosophy of language. Whether the opposite is also possible, I leave to the philosophers to decide.

Both have one thing in common: the enemy. Both are fighting against the opinion of Faust which has today become the dominant one that speech is man's instrument. Both are fighting the positivistic notion that meaning and power and deed and above all fact are more important than the mere powerless empty word.

According to the modern notion, which had already appeared with the Greeks, speech is a means by which people make themselves understood, in the words of Heidegger "planned in the whole economy of performances by which a man makes himself". The word decides priorities. Speaking is to express what is inside, to reveal a reality which already exists but is hidden. *Legein*, speak, *logos*, means originally to read off, count up, reckon, distinguish, and above all make explicit. The *logos* reveals a situation. Its meaning lies in what is spoken, not in being spoken. The ground of its being is its meaning, not the time and place of its utterance. Speech is thought of as an instrument. As a mirror of the world, it puts the world at our disposal. As a means of communication it is a tool of productivity, and productivity spells its downfall as we learn in the story of the tower of Babel. The nature which is capable of forging and using this instrument is called the *zoon logon echon* ("the living being having the word"; rational animal), and this definition of man is very close to the modern anthropological definition which defines him as a "tool-making animal".

How can this instrument be made fit for use? Logic can answer our question, logic whose derivation is *logos*. The most exact form of expression is the concept. To express and make comprehensible is the work of the tool of speech, whose logical schema is the relationship between subject, verb and object.

The grammatical form of the parts of the sentence is independent in the Indo-Germanic languages from its factual content. I buy, I build, I love. The content has no grammatical role; I am the subject upon which objects depend. In unreflective languages such as Chinese, words which we distinguish as subject and object have an equal rank and our characteristic relationship between the doer and the receiver of the action is ignored. In some Australian languages, what we call the subject changes its case according to what it does. With verbs of possession it is genitive, with verbs of sensual apprehension it is dative, and so on. The subject-verb relationship is thus not formalized, the accusative object is missing.

These examples can make some things clearer to us about the Indo-Germanic languages. For our relating of all nouns which are not the subject to the subject presupposes our Western way of looking at the world which has found its natural expression in modern technology. Subject and object are the pillars not only of our speech but also of our thought. In the concept, the thing placed before us, the fixed object, we have the fullness of modern speech. Language is an instrument of domination over the objectifiable; it submits the world of *extensio* to the domination of *cogitatio*. Logic is simply the most radical form of this subjection. Language as a calculus, giving the most exact possible information, eliminating all remnants, guarantees man his dominion over his world, which is only suggested in less formal languages.

But if the meaning of a word is its usefulness as an instrument in the understanding of the factual, it follows that every non-instrumental word is empty talk. It is precisely this tendency, clarifiable by the philosophy of language, which makes things difficult for current theology. Its word becomes incomprehensible, not because it is too high, majestic or otherworldly, but because it is not an instrument for conveying information, it is "just" a word.

In John's gospel Peter says to Jesus, "Thou hast the words of eternal life". Only words, Faust would answer. Is that all? Where is the power, where are the deeds of eternal life? "I cannot rate the word so high." According to the modern definition the real is the objectifiable, that is to say everything capable of becoming an object. The words of eternal life can have a meaning when they are about a predetermined later date or an objective world beyond. For the moment they say nothing and the Church would be better off if Peter had said: Thou hast the factual proofs of eternal life!

The biblical talk of the word is senseless to an instrumental theory of speech. "Thy word is a lamp to my feet and a light to my way." Why does the psalmist not say, "Thy deed is my light"? Who can put his trust in such an invisible, transitory, perhaps deceptive thing as the word? How can a mere word, or, as Luther says, a pure word, have the power to lighten our way? Has God only a word to offer? Has he no facts? This question, often asked, reveals that positivistic ways of thinking do not only exist outside the Church. Even Lutheran theologians today are ashamed of the mere word, and think that events in the history of salvation are far more important.

For in positivisitic thought, philosophical, theological or unlearned, it is taken for granted that in every contest between word and fact, fact is the winner. We take this for granted to such an extent that a word which contradicts known facts can have no possible use for us. And yet there are such words, and if it can have any meaning to say that man does not live by bread alone but by the word, it follows that even the man who despises the word, the *misologos*, as Plato calls him, also lives by the word as he encounters it.

Jesus at any rate decided the contest between word and fact in favour of the word. Think, for example, of the story of the woman taken in adultery, who had been caught in the very act and who, according to the law, should have been stoned. The facts are plain, not only her action but everything about the woman makes it probable that she will go on being an adulteress. Jesus, however, speaks a word which contradicts the act she has committed, the judgment of the law, true psychology and all natural probability. He says, "Go and sin no more". Can his word possibly have more weight than the facts?

We must not weaken the case by saying: Well, of course, it was *Jesus* speaking. Jesus' word was not accompanied by thunder and lightning. There were no magical trappings to lend his word extra authority, any more than he had a halo round his head. Anyone who starts muttering about the almighty word in this situation does not know what he is talking about. Jesus' word was as little a thing as anybody else's. It did not have any greater force against the mighty fact. It was not a higher "heavenly fact", but simply a word, an empty word, as we call it.

Can a word have more weight than a fact? And if it ever can, what would this mean? Would it be a means of communication? Is Jesus informing the woman of his opinion of her case? Or is the purpose of his word something quite different?

Perhaps philosophy of language can give us some further help, for it too has been led through its phenomenological method to a non-positivistic conception of language. An instrumental theory of language sees the word as inferior to the fact. The factual is the real and we express it by opposing subject to object. The grammatical distinction between subject and object corresponds to the ontological distinction between essence and existence, the philosophical distinction between soul and body, the aesthetic distinction between form and content, the sociological distinction between superstructure and base, all of which distinctions are characteristic of modern thought. They are all called in question when the phenomenon of language is examined in an unprejudiced way, that is to say in a way not predetermined by a particular grammatical structure. But is such an unprejudiced examination possible? In order to prescind from the grammatical structure of our speech, would we not have to prescind from speech, whereas in fact it dominates all our thinking, as Jaspers has pointed out. This is where we need the philosophical examination of actual languages and a comparison between them to make it possible to consider our own language objectively. The dualism between subject and object cannot stand in the face of a phenomenology of language. The ontological distinction between essence and existence cannot stand, for speech does not and could not have an unspoken "essence" before it "exists". Speech must be spoken. God could not have thought it up before it was there any more than men first feel the need of it, then design it, then possess it as an instrument. The dualism between soul and body is also contradicted by speech. We cannot think or talk to ourselves without words which can be heard and spoken. The aesthetic categories of form and content are not capable of seeing language as poetry. And the socio-

logical distinction between superstructure and base can be
shown to be irrelevant by the phenomenon of speech. When
a doctrinaire Marxist like Stalin corrects the classical teaching
in which nothing exists outside this schema and demands a
special position for speech, this is proof of its power indeed.

Language defends itself against dualistic divisions which
seek to debase it to a mere means of conveyance. All great
thinkers about language have rejected a purely instrumental
concept of it. Hamann maintained that poetry and not prose
was the mother language of the human race—which did not
sound any less astonishing in his time than in our own. He
intended it as a safeguard against a prosaic-instrumental conception of language. Hamann pleads for the original world-
revealing word against the known fact which can only be
added to. If language were "prose" it would be merely a tool
within the world for the use of man. Modern linguistic
science makes this position a dubious if not impossible one.
Linguistic scholars, whether anthropological or philosophical,
now agree that the nature of speech is "hermeneutic", that is
to say explanatory. The linguistic art of interpretation is a
hermeneutic of the world achieved through language. We
experience the world, that is to say our knowledge of it, only
as we give it meaning, speak of it and understand it. A world
which has not been put into language is nothing. In other
words there is no unprejudiced immediate access to things,
and language, by which we apprehend, order and name things,
contains an exposition of being. There are not first facts and
then words for them but only a reality already expressed in
language. A summary of facts is itself an exposition of the
world, which is in no way nearer to reality than the non-statis-
tical thought of Jesus. We cannot get behind language.

This realization of the hermeneutical world-explanatory
function of language is extremely important for theology. For

its most disputed question at the moment is the problem of hermeneutics, the problem of interpreting in the correct and scientific way, and the ramifications of this problem become ever more extensive. At first hermeneutics was concerned with the proper interpretation of the biblical texts, a process that became increasingly difficult with the passage of time. Is it possible at all to understand the world of first-century Galilean fishermen, now so far in the past? Understanding the stories does not mean simply knowing what the people of those days did, thought and believed. It is more important to let this past speak to us, say something for our profit, offer us possibilities which we can accept or refuse. The detached observer gets nothing of this. He can learn facts but he does not understand them and they make no difference to him. In a genuine—we could also say, tautologically, existential—understanding the person who has understood is changed. What is strange, different and new in the past (or the present) becomes his own. He hears it as helpful or threatening, as offer or demand. Here we see the full extent of theology's hermeneutical problem, which began with an examination of texts. Not just how can I understand the Letter to the Romans? Or how can I understand the death and resurrection of Jesus? But how can I understand God? Is it possible to understand God? Has he spoken? And so, if we ask at all and are serious, we must ask, does he speak? When and where and how?

The centre of the hermeneutical problem is the search for the word in, with and behind the words. We can understand God because and in so far as his opinion is the opinion of the Bible. Theology must take its contents seriously if it is seeking, not for knowledge of God, but for understanding of him. The word knowledge now has connotations of natural science and in Greek thought it belongs together with "being". Knowledge makes what is known an object. The invisible God cannot be seen or known but he can be heard and understood. But can we understand him? Isn't this human presumptuousness? What does "word of God" mean anyway? First we must say a little more about present-day theology to show why it has this interest in language.

The dialectical theology of the 'twenties stressed that God encounters us as the wholly other, who gives man something quite new and unforeseeable, which he could not have got or even understood by his own powers, however highly he might develop them. The strangeness, we might also say the incomprehensibility, of God is for Karl Barth a condition of his godhead. Revelation differs from every human religion because in it God has the first word, which he puts to us, and not the other way round; his language is not our language, but a wholly other language which can only be heard and understood by faith.

But how can this wholly other God be heard if man has no link with him whatever? Does not his word then become a metaphysical foreign language only comprehensible to the initiate? Barth considered but did not solve the problem of natural theology, that is to say the question what has God to say to the non-Christian? We must hold with Barth that the word of God to man is something new which man could not find or speak for himself. The word must be heard. Faith is the only way to God.

But it is also true that this word must be understood. And for this the word must have already been expected and sought, even if in a completely wrong direction. Is man not always seeking the good life? He does not seek it in the word, for he has more trust in fact. Nevertheless he lives by the word and understands it.

Which comes first, faith or understanding? Liberal theology replied, understanding, dialectical theology replied, faith.

Rudolf Bultmann, who is largely responsible for the present theological situation, gave his work the programmatic title "Faith and Understanding". What is the meaning of the "and"? Is it the stairway between the ground floor and the first, natural and supernatural knowledge? Is it the station at which theologians who also believe and Christians who also want to think must change trains? Or should we see in this "and" a reference to language, to the word that demands both faith and understanding and unites them? It is surely not accidental that it was friends and pupils of Bultmann, Ernst Fuchs and Gerhard Ebeling, who raised the language problem to a theological issue of first importance.

The question of which comes first, faith or understanding, would then appear to be wrongly formulated, like the previous question about the priority of reality or word. The philosophical knowledge of the hermeneutical structure of language is relevant to the question of the meaningfulness of any language about God. Does God first *exist* and then *speak*? In that case he would still be thought of as an objective fact, as the highest being, as Heidegger says. But if God is encountered *as* word, better perhaps, if God happens *as* word, then there can be no question of first holding him to be true and then believing in him. He who goes along with the word of God, that is to say believes, understands God. Just as we cannot "get behind" language to an immediate and unprejudiced access to things, we cannot get behind the word to "God himself". God happens as word.

Which means in concrete terms that every atheist is capable of understanding the story of Jesus and the woman taken in adultery. And it need not turn him into a theist. In this story Jesus risks his word against the facts of the Pharisees and statisticians. Does God occur as word in this story, even though the story is not about God? Can one say that God occurs in this story? In that case the question we passed over earlier about the character of this word must be taken up again.

Let us turn again to the philosophy of language for help. It is agreed that there are three dimensions in the process of language. There is the speaker, what is spoken and the person spoken to. I say "It" to "You". The "I" gives "It" as a signal or communication to the "You". This is the semantic relation. If the cry of "Fire" is raised at midnight, this one word contains within it the self-expression of the "I" who is in danger or half burnt, the conceptualized "It" of the fire itself and the "You" addressed, the fire brigade. Of course these three dimensions do not appear in every sentence. Language can be an expression of feeling without seeking to communicate it, a kind of speech for its own sake; or it can abstract from both the I and the You, as in the sentence two and two make four.

Speech need not achieve its ultimate goal in either of these cases, it can be delayed, for example. Judgment is withheld, the stove will still be hot in the morning. But if one person addresses another or asks for something, a response must be made at the time of speaking. Is this mode of speech therefore primary? Opinions differ. Is speech the expression and the mirror of the I? Is it an instrument for conveying information in the form of the concept? Is it naming things? Has any of these functions ontological primacy? A philosopher can ask these questions and work out the consequences of the possible answers, but he cannot give a final answer. We can see how different ways of looking at the world place these dimensions in a different order. A linguistic theory orientated towards the Greek *logos* implies a scientific and technical view of reality. The word is understood by what it contains, it is a timeless word. The question what does the word achieve, where does it point, what future does it offer, does not arise. In Hebrew and biblical thought the word is not timeless and meaningful independent of its utterance, but addressed to the hearer. It creates new possibilities. It does not offer new information but it changes the hearer. It changes him not by giving new knowledge but by speaking to him with a threat or a promise. Production requires the instrumental word, art requires the word as a means of expression, but man requires the word as a means of address, which neither informs nor expresses him. He needs the word as a call and a question and a gift, the word that occurs now and opens the future to him.

Theological interest in speech is therefore not neutral. It is not on the side of the timeless but of the historical word, it is not on the side of the "I" or the "It", but the "You", it is on the side of man who does not live by bread alone but by the word which opens the future to him.

"Speak that I may see you," said Hamann, a thoroughly un-Greek expression. A Greek proverb says, "Eyes are better witnesses than ears", and the number of Greek words for "see" is far greater than for "hear", which is not the case in Hebrew. The Greek orientation towards the world is under the tutelage of the eyes. To render his expression in a Greek way Hamann would have to say, "Show yourself, come into the light, that I may see you". His paradoxical formulation passing from the dimension of hearing to that of seeing does the same thing as the psalmist who says the word is a light to his feet. The rather unhappy terms *Wortgeschehen*, word-happening (Ebeling) and *Sprachereignis*, speech-event (Fuchs) are trying to do the same. The German *Sprachereignis* keeps the link between the acoustic and the optic because the word *Ereignis* still reminds us of the ancient *Eraügnis* (*Augen* = eye) known to Goethe.

These expressions are decidedly against the notion that the word is something only subjectively valid, powerless and unreal. They are trying to say that between subjective opinion, pious sentiment as it were, and objective fact, the so-called salvation facts, there is a third possibility more real than either of the others which stresses the optical tendency of these words, and this is the self-fulfilling word.

We should not take even the word of Jesus when it contradicts the facts either as information or as the expression of his inner life. If we want to abstract a general teaching from this word, we have failed to understand him. The stove is still hot in the morning but this does not make "neither do I condemn thee" a universal truth. Jesus' word is addressed to a person. It is an example of the "You" dimension of speech. It promises, it addresses, it warns, it forgives. It does not communicate information about facts already in existence. It reveals what is not visible as invisible. It calls the future into being. It is not a means of communication, but itself a communication. It is not a means of life, but life. What it says is not independent of the person spoken to. It is speech *to* someone.

In every proper address to a particular person in a particular situation which is not transferable to other circumstances, a new possibility is revealed. It need not necessarily take the imperative form. The apparently informative turn of phrase "I tell you" does not give information about something already in existence which is then spoken about. But the event occurs in the speaking. It is not a feeling being clothed in words—as if words were simply clothes to be put on and off! Word is not opposed to deed but it decides the situation, it is itself an action. When we hear in the liturgy the words of Jesus, "Your sins are forgiven you", this does not need sacramental confirmation. The thing itself is not *behind* the word, as if the forgiveness of sins was a measurable fact, but the word itself has the power to change the situation radically, it can offer a future not open before, it can do precisely what we were saying in our hermeneutical problem, it can be an act of

God and give man something he could never have got for himself.

But is this not putting the human and divine word on the same level? In fact God's word occurs as any other word of mouth from man to man. There is no formal criterion by which it can be identified as divine. It makes no difference whether it comes from the government, the wireless or someone sitting in your kitchen, whether it is accompanied by "thus says the Lord", by thunder or by "In the name of the Father". This guarantees nothing. A lot of preaching goes on. Luther says, "Whenever God's word is preached it makes the conscience glad and clear and certain in its relation to God . . . but whenever the word of man is preached the conscience becomes sad, close and fearful". The criterion for the word of God is therefore the future it reveals. The word is shown to be the word of God when it makes men human, glad, open and certain. And a man who has been made free of his own humanity will no longer be dependent on another man for the true word. For the word comes in a way which makes it unnecessary to guard and preserve it in holy books. It must be kept alive, unguarded, and free to move. For why did the word become flesh unless to enable flesh to become word?

But if we call the word of God the "common" human word, we do not mean it is like the kind of word that most often passes between men. It is more usual for a man to deny the word that makes his way plain. One person can commit himself to another, and this is perhaps the highest word that we can speak because we offer our future to another, but we cannot do this "altogether", we cannot give another person salvation or even happiness. But it is also possible for one person to entrust another to God, as Jesus commits the woman taken in adultery to God when he says, "Neither do I condemn thee".

But how can one find God in order to entrust another person to him? Isn't this being rather brave? Faith answers this question with the promise God gives us in Jesus.

God in fact has nothing else to offer but his word. He does not make us sure of him by giving us facts that we could check. Even the resurrection of Jesus is not such a fact as they would have it be who trust a fact more than the mere word. But although the resurrection is our salvation, it is nonetheless not a fact that we can check. Or does salvation come in and through facts? Then Faust would be right, and in the beginning would be the meaning and deed and not the word. But must we be so radical? Can word and fact not coincide, first the facts which, second, mean salvation? The escape from positivism in theology which goes by the name of "existential interpretation" is only in its earliest stages. Objectifying thought wants to check its facts. Can love be checked? Is it that sort of fact? No, it is not. Is love and its word then unreal and irrelevant? Or is love and its word what is most real?

Jesus at any rate opposed to the facts only his word, not more powerful facts. The decisive fact against which he speaks his word we have not yet mentioned by name. It is death. In our story in John 8 two people should rightly die. First, the woman taken in adultery should, according to the law, be stoned. Second, Jesus should be condemned because he contradicts the law. The Pharisees bring the woman to him in order that they may condemn him. Jesus accepts the challenge and opposes his word to the facts. If death is the fact of facts, then love is the word of words. When Jesus risks everything in his word—love has only itself to offer—two things happen. His word becomes stronger than the fact, the woman taken in adultery is not stoned, his word of love prevents her death. But Jesus accepts his own death. For both are true, the word of love is stronger and it will be done to death while love still remains invisible. And God must decide whether man can live by the word or must live by the facts. God ratifies the act of Jesus by deciding the contest between the word of love and the fact of death in favour of the former. The word of love lives, it happens, it is spoken and it is heard. As this word, Jesus is raised from the dead. The story of love does not end on Calvary but begins there.

But the story of love remains the story of its word, its invisible, time-bound, self-fulfilling, promising word. "The Lord is hidden", says Luther. "Therefore he has placed love in the outward word and in our neighbour." So love is promised to us in the spoken word between men. It remains an event of speech. Because it is invisible it is waited for. Therefore its sister's name is hope. Because it is the pure word, it tells us about God. Now we may "translate it differently": In the beginning was love. And love was with God and God was love. Love was in the beginning with God. All things were made by it and without it nothing was made. In it was life and the life was the light of men.

9
Thou shalt not make to thyself any Graven Image

The purpose of the ten commandments is to protect a man from his fellows, and they are therefore best understood by a man who has not been protected by them. The man who has been robbed realizes the rightness and necessity of the commandment "Thou shalt not steal" better than any other man. There is no better testimony to the way the commandments protect life than the bitterness and hatred of those who have not been protected. The meaning of a commandment can best be seen in the man who has been deceived, not the liar; in the man whose wife has been taken, not the adulterer; in the murdered man, not the murderer; in the receiver, that is, rather than in the doer of the action.

We find it hard to understand the prohibition of graven images precisely because we cannot see who could be hurt by it. I should like to begin with an experience that everyone must have had because it is very common. I mean the experience of being pigeonholed, whether appropriately or not. Once when I had given a lecture a student who had been arguing with me said to me: "I understand you well. As a woman you would be bound to hold that position." I have nothing to say to him, I thought. He knows what a woman will think without my help. His picture is complete before I even open my mouth. This sort of thing is always happening. Because you are seventeen you must think in this way. We have all done

82

it. But whenever it happens, we are burying something, people's possibilities. I am established as a person who is not myself, or at any rate not all that I am. For it may be true that I always think in the prescribed way for a woman, a seventeen-year-old, a bourgeois, a German, and never free myself from the habits, desires and prejudices of my class, race or sex. But nevertheless the resulting image still does not cover all that I am. For I cannot be contained in pictures that were made before I even existed, and I am not only what other people know, expect and predict about me. The classifications of statistical probability cannot contain the living human being.

The image falls short of me, even though it may be correct in the details about me it gives. These are still only a partial truth. But in this case a half-truth or even three-quarters truth is a plain lie. And an image which sets me in a particular, clearly defined scene leaves out my ability to say to myself, "I could be different". I am more than any picture of me created by psychology, and not just quantitatively more but qualitatively different from the object of any science. The reason for this "more" is that I live in and with time. Because I am in time, or rather because I have time, not just the chronological passage of time but time in which to change, time which changes me, all images fall short. For an image allows me no future. Every attempt to say "this is what you are like" not only freezes me in the present but takes away all my future possibilities.

Images have power. This is what the second commandment is about, although it may sound like a relic from a time infinitely remote. In Mea Sharim, that part of the Old Town of Jerusalem inhabited by strict Jews, I once saw two old men with corkscrew curls on their temples having a conversation and gesticulating eagerly. A tourist tried to take a photograph of them and they immediately took off their caps and covered their faces. "Thou shalt not make to thyself any graven image nor the likeness of any thing that is in heaven above or in earth beneath or in the waters under the earth." The commandment is obeyed literally by orthodox Jews. Photography is not allowed. For an image is not seen as a lifeless object but as containing some kind of power.

All Israel's neighbouring States worshipped images in holy places as the bearers of divine virtue. What happened to the image concerned the divinity. Priests washed, fed and clothed the image, an abandoned image avenged itself, and a well-honoured image rewarded its faithful. It was an unforgivable sacrilege to damage an image of a god.

In Israel it was different. The anger of God fell upon the man who worshipped an image, or served it, that is to say performed rites of ritual cleansing, dance and song before it. The God of Israel did not allow an image to be made of himself. In the introduction to the second commandment it says: "You did not see any form on the day when the Lord spoke to you on Horeb out of the fire, so that you may not act shamefully and make an image of God." The invisible God does not want his virtue to be contained in an image, because in the image this virtue can be arrested, imprisoned, possessed and used. The ancient gods allowed themselves to be "used" through their images, their attitude could be influenced, once they had been arrested in an image. In the image the god surrenders, much as the two old Jews thought they would be surrendering themselves if they allowed themselves to be photographed. A photograph is a way of capturing them, of arresting them, from which they could not escape; to make an image is a way of seizing power over something in order to manipulate it.

The prohibition of images is for the protection of those whom the image seeks to turn into objects and rob of their virtue. The power of the image is therefore a magical power which we no longer understand today. But images are still dangerous and we should still beware of them.

The powerful image is no longer the cultic image which can be influenced by magic, but the presupposition, the cliché and the predetermined category. Images have power. The false category which seeks to determine my place is not only an error from which I can find my way out. It is also "a sin and a shame". For the image determines the future. A child who is branded as stupid becomes stupid. A film producer who thinks of his audience as tasteless and mindless, and tailors his film accordingly, contributes towards their tastelessness and mindlessness. The public accepts the role it is offered and the film is not only mindless but encourages mindlessness. A totalitarian régime not only behaves as if its subjects were mindless but also makes them so without any physical compulsion. He who has heard often enough that it is up to the rulers to think and plan ends up believing it. The image proves its power. And the maker of the image sees himself vindicated, he was right all along. From the beginning he betrayed the living future to the image.

Max Frisch describes the power of the image in a journal, which he later turned into a play. He tells the story of a young man in Andorra who is thought to be a Jew and who has to cope with the commonly accepted picture of the Jew. This image forms him, and forecloses his future by elbowing out all other possibilities. It enslaves the young man without the creators of the image realizing it. The Andorrans, for example, assume without question that a Jew thinks before all things about money. The young man considers the ready-made picture presented to him, he tests it and finds that in fact "it fits: he does think constantly about money". And this happens all the time. The fatherland appears inaccessible to him and so his attitude to it is critical and problematic. He is deemed incapable of being simple and jolly and so he only engages in partial relationships with other people. He is seen as an alien, he accepts the role and becomes an alien, as anyone else would have done. The end of the story in the play is that he is not really a Jew at all but an Andorran like all the others. His so-called typically Jewish characteristics are not inborn but acquired through his relationships and the images of him other people had. But this is not discovered until he has been foully slaughtered as a Jew in a pogrom. The image has proved its murderous power.

This example makes plain what is at stake in the second commandment. It is the reality of the unknown, the un-comprehended, the mystery of the person, not a soluble riddle but permanently mysterious. If we form an image of another person or seek to dismiss him with a classification, we are denying what is strange in him, what is unexpected and has not yet appeared. The image takes the place of the future and thus deprives the reality of its most important dimension. I am more than any image of me that purports to foresee my future actions, behaviour and feelings. The image does not tell everything about me. As Sartre puts it with startling simplicity, I am my freedom. This freedom is taken away from me by the image, even a friendly and well-meaning image. This too limits me and falls short of my reality. Frisch shows very well how even the "progressive" Andorrans, who are not anti-semitic, nevertheless fall short in their "image of the Jew". They only find in the young Andorran what they have come to think of as typically Jewish, they do not let him be what he is, they do not allow him his freedom.

The second commandment is one of the places in the Bible where an attempt is made to guard this freedom. It is not possible to form an image of a man without damaging him.

He cannot be fixed and classified according to the characteristics he displays. He cannot be defined by race, class, sex, education or environment. Of course these factors are important, but in Jewish and Christian thought we cannot say I am an employee, a German or a woman without also saying I am my freedom. We do not prove this freedom, it is simply "expected" of a rational being to think of himself in this way. It cannot be demonstrated. To hold the classifications—place, time, race, and so on—to be a sufficient way of describing a human existence is to have the confidence to make images and know how "the" Jew, "the" Communist, "the" refugee, does and will behave.

But God does not want such classifications. "Thou shalt not make to thyself any graven image." God, who according to the Bible issues this prohibition, thereby makes himself the defender of our freedom. He does not guarantee it, that is not like God. He does not promise it, as Jesus did later, but he defends it. God is on my side. This sentence should not be read as egoism but as the joy and gratitude of the creature who has been given his freedom. And of course it also means that God is on my brother's side.

If we shift our emphasis from the receiver to the doer, then our subject is not "my" freedom but "your" freedom, which I should preserve against—my own—incursions. God thinks so much of us that he entrusts us with the totally mysterious, the freedom of another person, which we can preserve if we give up trying to categorize him. God seriously expects it of us. He leaves us with a free future. God thinks more highly of us than we do of ourselves, but this is always so when there is love; he gives us this dangerous freedom in our relations with our fellow men. He entrusts us with himself.

Thou shalt not make to thyself any graven image. But it happens all the time. Perhaps there is no other commandment so often sinned against in thought, word and deed. We categorize endlessly. We make plans for our neighbours and everyone else. There is only one way to escape, and keep the commandment. Max Frisch ends his story with the words: "It is a sin that we commit almost ceaselessly, except when we love."

10

We do not know what we should pray

"Know your situation, take your failings into account, use your assets" (Gottfried Benn). "We do not know what we should pray" (Paul). Is there any possible connection? Know your situation. Paul gives the situation: We do not *know* what we should pray. Use your assets. Paul considers assets: We do not know *what* we should pray. Knowledge of the situation and an account of its assets are the work of philosophy and sociology today. Man's alienation from himself is the account of the situation given over a hundred years ago by Karl Marx. Sociologists consider the assets as scope for planning. Has the apostle Paul anything to say to this society? What have his words to say to us in the present? They are taken from Romans 8.26. Can we understand what Paul means? Whom does he mean by "we", anyway? We do not know what we should pray. Three chapters earlier he speaks of the same "we". "Justified by faith we have peace with God." He is not referring to the Jews or to the Greeks, about whom he was speaking earlier on, or to the Communists, materialists, believers in God, and so on, but to the members of the Christian community. Know your situation. Paul describes the situation of a Christian in Corinth whence he is writing, and in Rome where his letter is bound, by saying: We do not know what we should pray. In the year A.D. 57 or 58 Christians were people who did not know what they should pray. Does this mean that this is the situation of the Christian at all times?

We do not know what we should pray. The sentence is not a timelessly valid statement which could always be taken in the same way and once understood remains the inalienable possession of the human mind. On the contrary, it demands that we should consider a particular situation. We try to come to know ourselves through Paul, and review our assets. Is it still true today that we do not know what we should pray? And if so, in what sense is it true?

Know your situation. To whom is this command addressed? Doubtless Gottfried Benn did not intend it for the Christians but for his contemporaries of agnostic or liberal stamp. Could Paul help him to reach a correct assessment of the situation? It sounds a stupid idea, for how would it help in the understanding of our modern world to go back to a community which was at any rate only a pretty dim minority? To suggest it would be pure arrogance! Is it possible for a Christian to assess the situation in a way that would have general validity? Is there such a thing as a Christian assessment or only good and bad assessments? In fact theology claims to make statements not only about the Christian community but about all men in the world, that is to say to give a good assessment of the general situation. It claims to consider the reality of man, before he is divided into believers and unbelievers. Is this possible? We cannot yet answer this question and must lay it aside. We must beware of a too facile distinction between world and Church. Is it a tenable distinction?

Make use of your assets. Let us try to do so. Paul has few assets to show. Clearly the Christians are not people to whom "religion" comes easily. Such people know what they should pray. Believers on the other hand do not know, they have no prayer ready made, as Paul admits. Why is this? Is there no such thing as immediacy of religious fervour which can always find words old and new in which to express itself? But at the time Paul wrote, the Christians of Rome and Corinth did not know what they should pray. Did they know before they became Christians? Did Paul know when he was still called Saul? But as Paul he writes: We do not know what we should pray; to pray as we ought the Spirit himself intercedes for us. Could Saul have written this sentence? He did not need anyone to intercede for him. He prayed, as he ought; he was a pious Jew and did not need the help invoked by Paul the Christian. To pray means first of all to belong to the household of a religion. He who knows what he should pray, how it should come, what is necessary, has a roof over his head. The roof of the house in which he grew up. The special times, the direction to face in, the attitude of the body, the special gestures and words, all these are summed up in the expression "as we ought". These prescriptions are common to all religions. Scientific research into prayer, as conducted by G. van der Leeuw in his phenomenology of religion, comes to the conclusion that prayer is originally "the exercise of power". The power lies in the particular sacred word, which is spoken at a particular time, in a consecrated place in a prescribed manner. This form of prayer, which is bound to a particular form of words and seeks to exercise power, is "praying as we ought", the necessary act of piety. Paul has lost the knowledge of it.

Religion as the house which protects a man, the roof built by his fathers and which his sons will continue to preserve, no longer exists. The immediate prayer available to the members of this household has become impossible for Paul. He no longer knows what he should pray, as he ought. It is not an accident that the early Christians were described by their heathen neighbours as *atheoi* or godless. They had left the house in which dwelt many worshippers of the gods. Christianity was not thought of as a religion. The Christian way of worshipping God made people irreligious. Religious people know what they should pray. With Christ the era of religions which know what they should pray comes to an end. Jesus turns people out of the house into the open. Luther describes this evicted man with an image, taken from the psalms, of the lonely sparrow on the roof. "He is alone and no one is with him for everyone is asleep. And (the psalmist) says on the roof as if he were to say that the world is a house in which all the people lie asleep but I am on the roof alone outside the house, neither in heaven nor on earth, hovering in loneliness between earthly and heavenly life."

One might almost take this loneliness of which Luther speaks as a form of the new subjectivism. The experience of the modern man who no longer lives in the house of religion is quite different from Luther's, because it does not bring with it loneliness but something more like a common isolation. And yet I think that this image of the bird alone on the roof, neither in heaven nor on earth, expresses the true Christian experience that the house of religion no longer protects us. To be in the house with other people and asleep is to have religion. For religion joins earth to heaven so that the heaven loses its frightening emptiness, whereas the bird on the roof is not at home in heaven either. Religion joins earthly to heavenly life by making the eternal present through liturgy and prayer, but it also shuts it up in a house and separates it from the profane things which lie outside the sanctuary. But Luther does not speak of the joining of earth and heaven but of being in a state of suspension in which one lives neither an earthly nor a heavenly life. Luther's man has no security. Hovering is an image of the state of being between earth and heaven. This transitional state, this hovering, Luther calls faith.

The man who no longer knows what he should pray is outside the house. Let us consider once more for a moment what it means to say that Jesus turns people out of the house into the open. In Jesus' preaching there are no more rituals; debates with the Pharisees on this issue take up a lot of space in the gospels.

God no longer encounters man in the house of religion. What did this house mean to him? If prayer originally meant to exercise power, it was an attempt to control an even stronger power. The stronger power is conceived as far away, threatening and elusive. Ritual actions and prayers seek to bring God near. The idea is to make God present through holy vessels, actions, words or persons. God's presence must be conjured up.

Now it becomes plain why Jesus no longer needs to keep people in the house of religion. God does not have to be made present, he *is* present. Religion seeks to overcome the gulf between God and man. But for Jesus this gulf no longer exists. God is out in the open, or, to be more precise, out in the open on the road between Jerusalem and Jericho, even though he is overlooked by the priest and the Levite and only noticed by the Samaritan. No place can be more sacred than the place where the man who fell among thieves lies helpless and thirsty. No time is more solemn and closer to God than the time when people pass by him in his need. No words could be more pious than the Samaritan's careful instructions to the innkeeper. "Take care of him and if you spend any more I will repay you when I come back." If it is true that God is the most important person in this story, even though his name is not mentioned, it follows that there is no more need for ritual to make him present because he is already there. Jesus sends man out into the open because that is where God is, not in a special place but in the everyday life of every man.

Because Jesus sends man out into the open, the house of religion has become uninhabitable for Paul. If we are to assess our situation, the first thing we can learn from Paul is that the age of religion is over for the Christian, and his proper place is to be in a state of suspension between earth and heaven.

But Paul is not only ignorant of *how* we should pray, of what form our prayer should take, he is ignorant of the content it should have. What used to be said will no longer do. *What* should we pray? Can this question be asked seriously? Is it not enough that we should pray at all? Health, peace, justice, help in all kinds of difficulties, all these Paul prays for in other places in his letters. So he often knows quite well what he should pray. So what does he mean here? He does not say we do not know what we should pray *for*. This we usually know quite well. Every petition has its point. But Paul joins the verb to the plain accusative, we do not know *what* we should pray. Whom or what should we pray? The answer can only be ourselves. To pray myself means to express myself. And this is difficult. Precisely because we know so well what we should pray *for*, we do not know *what* we should pray. We do not know how to express ourselves. But can *we* really be the content of our prayer? Are we ourselves what is harder to pray for than any petition? Is this not sheer egoism?

But when I myself speak to God, I speak in my *world*. To express myself to God does not mean a private relation to God, but to express God's world to God. So Paul uses the plural, *we* do not know. Were we to pray for the former chaplain to the Leipzig students because he was in prison, it would have to be the true prayer of our own self. We would be telling God about our world in which such a thing happens, our world in which God is so little visible, our world that needs him.

"Everything for others, nothing for myself" is therefore not a Christian saying. Is there anyone who has no need to pray for himself? Who does not need to express himself? If we consider the prayer of Jesus, this false notion will be corrected.

Corrected it reads, get back on the ground. Jesus who prayed for children, for his murderers, and for his disciples, teaches us first of all to pray ourselves. In the *Our Father* we speak of ourselves, we whose Father is in heaven and whose name and kingdom and will we need, but do not possess, we the hungry, guilty and trespassed against. The content of our prayers is therefore ourselves. The *Our Father* tries to express *us*.

This is how Jesus teaches us to pray and this is how he prays himself. In Gethsemane and on the cross he prays himself. "Why hast thou forsaken me?" Jesus' prayer does not leap up to heaven, but remains with him, it is humility, not self-possession, it is the request that this hour might pass from him. He who speaks like this is the real man.

The real man expresses himself in prayer. The mystics conceive of prayer somewhat differently. Tauler says: "Prayer is simply the surrender of the heart and mind to God". The word "surrender" here plays a twofold role. The heart and mind go up to God, and they are given up to God, or, as another mystic says, they become God-coloured. Both the way and the goal, the movement and the rest, are covered by the one word. But Jesus does not pray that he should cease to be himself, a man who needs help. If Tauler thinks the purpose of prayer is to lose oneself in God, Jesus does not; he remains himself in the presence of God. Tauler's goal is silence, for he who rests in God no longer needs to call upon him. The highest form of prayer is wordless. But this is not so with the real man from Nazareth and his brothers, of whom Luther says that they are hovering between earth and heaven. To put this state into words is praying. But we do not know how to put ourselves into words.

The era of religion comes to an end with the advent of the real man. But this fact was not commonly realized until eighteen hundred years later, at the time of the enlightenment.

The second point in Paul's account of the situation was that we do not know *how* to pray. What we lack is the language. Is this relevant to us? We could start by considering the words we used to pray in the house of religion. The word Father, for example, has become for a writer like Thornton Wilder entirely unsuitable as a way of talking about God. It makes God too comfortable and undemanding. The unsuitability of many ancient Christian terms to express what we want to say is a sign that language fails us, a sign of a problem far deeper than the old-fashioned sound of these words. In church we begin prayers after the sermon often with the formula "We thank thee". This also seems to be a formula which says nothing for us. The "we" presupposed is the community which has received the benefits, their contentment expresses itself as gratitude. If we accept the synoptic account it seems that Jesus was not nearly so pious as his Church. It is amazing how little he praises and thanks, that is, makes use of the higher forms of prayer, and how often on the other hand his prayer is petition.

Jesus waits, the Church possesses. Jesus asks, we say thank you. Paul does not know how he should express himself to God, but we know very well. We are not recommending ingratitude but humility. If we are looking for a language in which we can express ourselves, gratitude of the *beati possedentes*, the blessed possessors, helps us not at all. How often we put into our prayers not ourselves but an image of ourselves, dressed up, free from desires, and too noble for hopes. Where can we find a language which will express *us*?

We do not know how to express ourselves. This is neither the fault of the words themselves nor of the Church. The difficulty is to put the experience of the world which makes us what we are into words. A rather uncertain word to describe our uncertain condition would be ambivalence. We do not

speak and perhaps cannot speak of the disappointment of our
expectations, our gratified wishes which turn out to be boring,
our anxieties, or of anything important or enriching in our
lives. So we remain silent, for the ambivalence of our reality
involves us in an endless dialectic or leads us to say nothing
at all because we cannot say anything plain. Ambivalence
entrenches itself in silence and we do not know what we
should pray. Can ambivalence express itself without leaving
one half out of account? Perhaps a deeper reason for our
silence is our fear. For to speak, to pray, to express ourselves
would mean first looking at ourselves as we are. But this
frightens us. We become resigned and less and less able to
talk, as if we had no one left to talk to.

Lack of words, self-deception, inability to accept ourselves,
the ambivalence of our reality, unwillingness to ask, this is it:
we do not know how to express ourselves. Whereas a sage like
Confucius could confess in the abandonment of his scepticism:
Unfortunately we do not know what to pray, it would be a
mistake to read Paul in this way and take it that he was recording a fact. Paul is not recording a fact, he is complaining. But
the complaint is not against all comers but against one person in
particular. Do you remember the story of the goose girl? She
is really a princess and she has sworn to tell no one how she
came to change her state. She complains of the suffering,
which she may not betray, to her horse Fallada and then to the
iron stove. Which only goes to show that all complaints need
a hearer of some kind, even if it is only the iron stove. If it has
no hearer at all, then it ceases to be a complaint and becomes
the recording of a fact.

If there is no one to complain to and our words fall into the
empty void (but praise God there is no such thing in a fairy
tale: there is always an iron stove), we must give in to resignation. Complaint needs the dative predicate, we need to be

G

able to say we do not know how to express ourselves to you. So we must correct our first formula "we have no language", for it suggests that a language could come out all on its own without anyone to listen. The sentence would only be in the mind of the subject and our object would be—the language itself. We have no language. Would everything be fine if we did? Is it possible to have a language at all? Would we then simply "have language"? Language which can be "had" is a means of communication. But the language whose lack Paul complains of is something else. We do not lack a means of communication, but communication. Language in this sense is not a means of communication but communication. "Word" as the reformers understood it is not a statement about something which can exist before there is anyone to receive it but it is addressed to someone, it is a message. The word "I love you" is not the communication of a previously established fact but an event which happens now in the present. An emotion is not being clothed in language but the word determines the situation. It is not the expression for something but an action, the exercise of power. The "fact" is not hidden somewhere behind the word, but the word announces the fact, it is annunciation and proclamation, not statement. So we must correct our formula "we have no language," because it treats language as an object.

Let us translate our sentence "we do not know what we should pray" with a phrase of Hölderlin's quoted by Heidegger: "Since we became a conversation we exist for each other and are listeners for each other." If the sentence "we have no language" will not do, we can say "we are not a conversation". We do not express ourselves because we are not listeners for each other. We do not answer because our words would not be heard. We do not live in dialogue. It is not the language we lack but we *are* not the dialogue we are meant to be, according to Paul. Speech without a listener is monologue, as we can see in certain plays of Ionesco. The sentence "we have no language" leads us at worst to the monologue of a person still capable of speech, we only reveal the full gravity of our state when we express it "we are not a conversation". If we try to become a conversation, then even when we are not being one everything is different.

So let us translate Paul's account of the situation, "we do not know what we should pray", with our new sentence "we are not a conversation". We are no longer complaining about the weakness of our connections but that there is no one to talk to us. "We do not know what we should pray" means that we hear nothing. Hearing and speaking go together, it is the proper relationship. Prayer does not seek a hearing as if we had the first word, but prayer comes from hearing. He who prays does not await an answer but is answering the word he has heard. The other does not then appear because he was already there, or rather he appears anew because he was already there. Only what is already there can come into the open and love suffers for the "long dead times". "Alas in long dead times you were my sister or my wife."

And so prayer becomes no longer a decision of the subject to speak but a conjunction of speaking and hearing. "Since we became a conversation" is saying the same thing as "since we became a prayer". And this brings us much closer to Paul. Praying is not a despairing cry to the empty heavens but an answer to the word, a response which is not something I have and give but something I am. A despairing cry is only possible because God is already there. Our whole life consists of despairing of an answer and seeking an answer. And therefore prayer, which is the attempt to express myself to God, cannot be confined to special times and formulas. We can pray without joining our hands. To pray is to direct our lives to God in response to his word. It is not, therefore, an occasional occupation but one that determines all we do.

And yet it remains true we do not know what we should pray. But to whom does Paul say this? To the Romans? I think he says it to God. Then his sentence would not be the recording of a fact, a statement, but an appeal, a cry for help. To say we do not know what we should pray *is* a prayer. Paul takes upon himself the poverty of those without religion, the homeless, who are not secure in their possession of the faith, the poverty of the insecure who are dismayed by the ambivalence confronting them.

Who are we? We asked Paul. Let us now ask ourselves. The barriers between belief and unbelief are broken down. Those who are not a conversation but yet acknowledge this, because they do not rely upon themselves, "we" who cannot pray, are saved. Paul prays by admitting that he does not pray. We do not know what we should pray, as we ought. We can no longer pray ritually, within a religion; we cannot make petitions because we need to be able to speak ourself to God. This speaking cannot be grateful, it asks and sighs, it has not yet received. We can only complain. A complaint needs a hearer, but before this the complainant must have heard himself.

How can we become a conversation? How can we learn to pray? I will end with a promise from Second Isaiah, chapter sixty-five, verse twenty-four. It is not a saying of the prophet but a saying of God, a promise which answers our question. "And it will come to pass that *before* they call upon me I will answer, and while they are yet speaking I will hear."

II

Church outside the Church

We all know people who do not belong to any Church but who nevertheless do not deny the Gospel. We all know people, and are perhaps sometimes among them, who only make use of their church membership on very special occasions, the great festivals, for example. We all know the so-called "marginal Christians". Of course the boundaries are very difficult to draw and only the very dogmatic can decide easily where church membership begins and ends. But clarity on this point bought at the expense of blindness to the changing reality. If we talk of "marginal Christians" we must have a schema at the back of our minds which can quite easily be put down on one sheet of paper. The centre is Christ and around him in a circle stand his community. On a wider circle are the others, in a confused relationship to the Church. And outside this wider circle stands the world and her children.

This picture is theologically inaccurate. Christ is not the centre point protected from the world by the Church. He is still present today where Jesus of Nazareth was to be found 2,000 years ago, among the publicans and sinners, the marginal Christians and the atheists. Why did Jesus consort with these people? Because he did not assess people by their habits or their views on God and immortality but by their expectations. And expectations of the kind which we still need to describe exist both inside and outside.

The words "outsider" and "insider" correspond to a

particular view of the Church, which is chiefly interested in
defining the Church in relation to the world. However, many
people belie this schema, they are neither inside nor outside,
and their relationship to the Church is too complicated and
strained to be defined by facile spatial metaphors. It is as if the
Church were a room for living in, in which everything of
importance happens. Outside, the world is cold and clear and
useful. Inside, the higher reality takes place and nothing outside can call it in question.

Such a Church might well attract the longings of the dis-
orientated but it cannot cope with their real difficulties in
faith and life. For it can only take seriously what goes on
between its four walls. The ecclesiastical resistance to the
Third Reich did not begin at the time of the persecution of the
Jews and the Socialists but only when the Church itself began
to be persecuted, and the Arian edicts were put into force
against it. Inside and outside then and now were all too clearly
distinguished. Inside there reigns another law still bearing
the marks of its pre-democratic origins and still censoring any
opposition. Inside there is now another view of authority,
regarded as highly questionable outside. Church and world are
so sharply divided in common speech and that Church is
made to sound like the real and better world, rightly preserving
itself from the threatening external dangers.

The main points in the structure are boundaries, danger,
fear. The great enemy, the devil in ever new shape, is the
world. The Church is always ready to forget that Christ has
got the power over the dominions and that his victory is not
just personal salvation for the individual but he has also changed
the face of the world. We may remark in the last two hundred
years that the situation of the Church has become more and
more complicated, with the progress of secularization. She
can no longer rely on the ancient pre-scientific fear-bound

imaginations. She is losing her authority, her dominant position, she has become one power among many, and must therefore defend herself! She defends herself externally by virtue of claims to power which bear more or less weight according to the political situation. Internally she deals with her loss of authority by trying to preserve an outdated social structure. She proclaims that a part of the world, the past world, is unassailable and not subject to historical change. Then she bullies people to perform certain tasks which are made into conditions of membership of the Christian community. Somewhat unwillingly, she builds her walls and demands a way of life whose style and social norms and image are necessarily bourgeois. She demands, which is worse, the sort of community adherence which can no longer be expected, since people have less and less desire for this kind of thing. She demands, finally, that people should be interested in an ancient document, the Bible. These demands clearly constitute high walls. They are attempts to arrest the progress of secularization, at least in this area. It is a hopeless undertaking.

When I was a child I was told that a Christian is a person who goes to church. When I grew up I found that Christ is not only in church. He lives and works in the world unobserved, is present where people's lives have become more real and free, and is crucified there where people's lives are in danger; and that has always been so. We can no longer ignore the presence of the "greater Christ" in the world, if we really believe that Christ died for all men. In Christ God has made us free, broken down the boundaries so that the official Church is no longer the only place to seek and believe in Christ. Isn't the "Church outside the Church" simply a consequence of secularization, a hidden Church, in which Christ is present unrecognized as on the road to Emmaus?

Surely faith in Christ appears today not only in the official

Church but also outside it. It appears where people's lives begin to be free or even expect to be free. It appears where people are willing to suffer and hope for this kind of life, have not given up asking questions about it and are not satisfied with cheap solutions, the common way of betraying the kingdom of God. When people are waiting for the kingdom of God, then Christ is with them even though they do not name his name. When people have buried their hopes, either under cheap and readily available satisfaction or under cheap good fortune which they already possess, then Christ is buried with them. The measure of the hidden Church is its hope. It is the expectant Church.

Nothing reveals a man's nature more than the hopes he bears and which bear him. If the name of Christ was no longer mentioned at all, the expectations and desires which showed on a human face would be witnesses to his presence in the world. Hope is greater since Christ came, and so is despair, and people who hope and are disappointed force us to abandon our strict division between inside and outside.

There are communities which arise only because of the situation and there are people who join together in order to turn waste ground into playing fields. As these undertakings can fail, so can the Church. But the hidden Church consists of people who are not consciously united, are not publicly active, who seldom or never go to church because they cannot see what good it would do but who nevertheless are involved in the movement, even if only through their expectations. They are perhaps interested in religion, they may listen to religious broadcasts or read books written by Christians, may even like what they read but never go on to consider committing themselves to a Church, they are post-Christian humanists living somewhere between anguish and self-salvation.

But we must ask now where we are to set the limits between

the hidden Church and the non-Church. What distinguishing factors could we cite so as not to give the impression that we are calling the whole world the hidden Church? The distinguishing factor is expectation and all the action and suffering that follows from it. In our country there are children in orphanages who do not do well because they are never visited on Sundays or other visiting days. There are also solitary women who visit a child every day for years and so give him the most important experience a human being can have: acceptance and acknowledgement of need. Whoever cannot see that this has something to do with Christ, cannot know Christ. This life which is needed and cherished does not arise out of our own powers for good, but it is a gift. To experience grace means to be capable of returning love. It does not make the least difference whether Christ is mentioned by name. The name of "God" is not mentioned in Jesus' story of the good Samaritan. But whenever this story is re-enacted, in the Congo, Alabama or Siberia, Christ is present, who first told of it.

Wherever people have to do with Christ, there is the hidden Church. They may not be ecclesiastically or even consciously having to do with him, but he is present anonymously. He who gives food or drink to the least of his brothers, or visits and comforts him in prison, accepts him and brings him closer to a more human life, does this to Jesus, as he himself said.

Of course we still have to ask why all these good people do not want anything to do with the Church. Have people really got something against faith in Christ or only against the institution whose purpose is to preach this faith?

Or better: is it in the nature of their hope to remain "outside" and must this Church remain hidden in the modern world? Or does the official Church offer no place for this expectant Church? The Church outside the Church is not a defaulting group which must be brought back to the fold at

all costs. This is not the proper mission to the latent Church.
For the Gospel itself teaches that people live and suffer in the
world in hope and self-sacrifice without it being necessary
for them to be official members of the Church. Man is not for
the Church but the Church for the world and she has no right
to dragoon people.

But on the other hand it is true that the unofficial Christian
has been driven out of the official Church because he did not
find a place in it. And this should disturb us. The Church, we
may remark socio-psychologically, is a place of disappointment. She insists that she should convert people to the way of
life and structure of piety she offers within her gates. People
do not ask today whether a man is a Christian but whether he
is "committed to a Church". The Church offers answers to
questions people do not think to ask, and inappropriate
groups and meetings that do not correspond to their normal
life, of which she is often ignorant.

And so these millions of people will have nothing to do with
the Church, they may belong to the hidden Church outside the
house, independent of the community and its public confes-
sions. The ancient definitions are no longer adequate to
describe this Church consisting of the visible and the invisible.
It will not do to say that the Church is Christ existing as a
community. For Christ is often anonymous and hidden. It
will not do to say that the Church is what preaches the true
Gospel, for we must take the working of the Gospel seriously.
It is through the preaching of this very Gospel that the world
has been transformed and become secular, and this means
that Christ is also preached and believed where his name is
never mentioned.

However true it is to say that this anonymous form of
Christianity is a phenomenon of our post-Christian times, it is
nevertheless also true that it has firm foundations in the

Gospel. The people who were waiting for Christ and put their hope in him were not members of some sort of pre-Church and did not always belong to the circle of disciples.

It is not true that the question of the hidden Church does not arise in the New Testament. The Councillor Joseph of Arimathea, the Syrophoenician woman with her sick daughter, the Roman centurion from Capernaum and the cultured Pharisee Nicodemus all belong to the expectant Church, and perhaps this pre-ecclesial situation in which Jesus went about and found faith and gave the Gospel to the world is a more useful picture than the official one of typical community piety. He who seeks the answer from Jesus himself must accept that Christ lives where people believe and hope and love, whether inside or outside the Church.

And so today as well as the official sermon we have a less direct form of preaching to the world, which may even be wordless. It bears witness to Christ even when his name is not mentioned. God happens, and silently, in what happens between people and the Gospel takes the form of expectation, word and deed, in which his name does not appear.

In March 1965 a white woman was shot in Selma, U.S.A. She was a housewife and the mother of six children, and she was shot because she had taken part in a protest march against racial discrimination. This fact is a part of the Gospel of Jesus Christ, it is the good news of love which was destroyed for the sake of another. Anyone who hears this news is not only shaken and enraged, he is also called upon to believe. He experiences what it is to do something for someone else, and he will know that we have a reason to hold fast to our vision of a better and a freer world.

The Church is also outside the Church. We cannot rest with this knowledge. It is our task to contribute towards a better understanding between the public and the hidden Church. The

future of the Church depends on what happens to these divid-
ing walls. The future of the Church depends on her capacity to
criticize herself and change.

The wall between the manifest and the hidden Church is
still all too solid. But people on both sides of the wall are
facing towards each other. Both forms of Christian existence
that we find in the world, and with which we must calmly
reckon, are dependent on each other.

How much do people in the hidden Church need the
official Church? Or can they do without it altogether? It may
seem quite unnecessary in individual situations. But what the
hidden Christian lacks is the lasting comfort given by the
continued preaching of the Gospel. The Gospel is a part of the
continuity of the person, provides context, and tells the story
of love in the world.

But this also means that the preaching is demanded of the
official Church. It is for her to find the language with which to
speak. It is for the official Church to give the comfort of the
Gospel and the criticism of the cross to the hidden Church;
and she often fails. And there is nothing the Church needs more
than the people in the hidden Church, their awareness, their
imagination and their capacity for hope. So far she has not
been very successful. As long as the Church does not do everything she can to offer a place to the modern, democratic and
critical consciousness, people will go on leaving the Church.
Their vitality is withdrawn because it is not used and does not
find what it needs in the Church. The hidden Church is a
warning to the institutional Church. Because the official
Church does not have a monopoly of Christian life, it may well
lose all those members to whom it could offer human and
spiritual help. Because the official Church is the visible institution it is for her to acknowledge and change the relationship.

Let me end with a story that you all know. A man had two

sons. There is the elder brother, the solid citizen, who knows his Bible and prayer book and has clear and fixed ideas about the proper way to live. Then there is the younger brother who was unable to get on at home and so launched himself disastrously into the world. But it is this younger brother that the father goes out to meet and take in his arms.

We may compare the Church today to these two brothers, both lost. And the Father still goes out to meet his lost son and takes him in his arms. It is conceivable that the elder brother might also allow his father to meet him.

If he had more insight he could recognize the hidden Church in his younger brother. He could discern in the blank faces of people who believe in nothing the hope of a world still waiting for Christ. If he accepted his younger brother without first demanding that he should adopt his way of life, he himself would become a different person. Reform can only come by accepting the younger brother, by the destruction of all prejudices, the renunciation of all fears, in the assurance that Christ is greater than his official house, that we meet him in the younger brother whom the Father accepted long ago.

The gospel of the two sons has an open ending. Jesus does not tell us how the elder brother behaved when his father told him to be glad about his younger brother. Is it possible for our Church to give this story a happy ending?